GENDER WITHOUT IDENTITY

AVGI SAKETOPOULOU

AND

ANN PELLEGRINI

For Ory.
And for the marvelous children like him.

EDITOR'S NOTE

My pleasures in publishing this book are poly-morphous.

As the founder of The Unconscious in Translation, my dominant pleasure is pride, a pride readers of the book will immediately understand. Most importantly the pride that as solidly as a book can be, as solidly as intellectual work can be, this is a contribution to making our world a better place.

My pride and my pleasure in their ideas are doubled by the clarity of their writing. Much as I value our fundamental metaphysical categories and concepts like *sublation* and *overdetermination* and the *interpenetration* of opposites, whenever possible Saketopoulou and Pellegrini are more likely to use words and concepts like *complexity* and *nuance*, like *growth* and *flourishing*.

As a member of the Conseil Scientifique of La Fondation Jean Laplanche - Nouveaux Fondements pour la Psychanalyse, my dominant pleasure lies in the ways this book furthers the goal of the Foundation: "to contribute to the development of psychoanalysis in France and abroad, in the spirit that inspired the scientific life of the founder."

Finally, this book provides me the surplus pleasure of repaying in small part the kindness shown to me by Jean and Nadine Laplanche.

—Jonathan House M.D.

The time has come to abandon slogans and think on our own.

—Jean Laplanche

CONTENTS

A BOOK THAT WAS NOT TO BE

When I invoke the question of ethos, I'm calling attention to...a very different conception of ethical behavior than one that proceeds from ethical rules or first principles and [that] features a moral agent who has maximal agency and unmitigated choice in the actions they take. An ethos emerges from an ensemble of practices; when we shift collective practice, we reconfigure ethos. Practices of care are always part of an emergent ethos. Because care isn't abstract, but only ever manifested through practice— action, labor, work—it is integral to our ways of doing.

—Hil Malatino, *Trans Care*

THE BOOK'S ORIGIN

WE DIDN'T SET OUT TO write a book. We were forced to by repression. Or, to be more precise, we were driven to complete this volume out of sheer determination to do something about the repression we were met with during the summer of 2022. We mention this from the top for two reasons. First, because it's important to articulate that while, yes, psychoanalysis is improving, repressive forces are alive and well in our field—not covert, not subtle, not indirect, but unambiguous, unambivalent, categorical. Second, the process of this volume coming into being mirrors some of the very processes we theorize in its pages: it is in the nature of the human being to "treat" experiences that are difficult, painful, even traumatizing. Out of that treatment can arise self-theorizations—in this case, psychoanalytic theorizations—that are not efforts to cope with or to survive trauma, but that, to the contrary, take up the energies roused by trauma to invent something new.

In saying this, we are taking an unusual approach to trauma, asserting that trauma produces more than misery, even as misery is neither to be denied nor diminished. In that key, in chapter one we offer an in-depth discussion of the treatment of an atypically gendered 12-year-old child to suggest a rather forbidden and dangerous link: trauma may have a share in the constitution of queer and trans life. We will shortly explain why we dare this risky theorizing, why we feel it is urgent and necessary, and why such a link is neither transphobic nor does it have to tip into conversion practices—all points fleshed out in depth in the first chapter.

Our book is committed to a form of thinking that helps psychoanalysts build a tolerance for how trauma can get spun *into* the subject, and to show how such "spinning" may have a share in the formation of non-normative gender and sexualities. As a psychic process, this spinning is not about consciously produced self-understandings or meaning-making that proceeds from a centered self. It is rather a more decentered process, having to do with how trauma forces the psyche to respond, which means that the psyche has to innovate and to invent. This invention is what we refer to as self-theorization. But we want to emphasize two things: First, such theorizations do not issue from a preexisting self; rather, self-theorization is critical to the constitution of subjectivity. Second, self-theorization is not the work of a volitional subject who consciously narrativizes the self. Self-theorizing, as we use it, arises as a response to being breached by the other, by *otherness*.[1]

If the connection we are making—that trauma may well be swirled into how one comes to be queer, sexually or gender-wise—is taken by some to equate to saying that queer life is somehow "broken" or in need of repair, this misinterpretation comes, in part, from restricted ways in which trauma is thought within psychoanalysis, including restrictions on which subjects and whose traumas psychoanalysis has traditionally been able or willing to think capaciously about. Generally speaking, such critical reflection has not been equitably extended to non-normative subjects—a point we'll return to shortly.

But first, here's the repressive backdrop against which

[1] In stressing these points, we are in sync with critical pressure that thinkers like Amin (2022), Dutta (2018), and Povinelli (2006) place on the liberal Western and colonial fantasy of individuals as fully self-determining beings.

this book was conceived: In June 2021 our paper, "A Feminine Boy: Normative Investments and Reparative Fantasy at the Intersections of Gender, Race, and Religion," received the first Tiresias Award from the International Psychoanalytical Association's (IPA's) newly composed Sexual and Gender Diversity Studies Committee (S&GDSC). We were more than personally delighted; we were aware of how much labor had been required for the setting up of S&GDSC within the auspices of the IPA. And, in fact, many analysts felt that the Tiresias prize was, politically speaking, a meaningful award. Interested in placing the winning papers in a reputable journal, the S&GDSC had discussed with the *International Journal of Psychoanalysis* (*IJP*), the oldest journal in the field— established by Freud himself—a path for the submission and possible publication of each year's Tiresias Award paper.

Accordingly, we submitted our essay to the *IJP*, where it was formally accepted, twice and in writing. We were offered the option of revising and took it, working closely with the journal's editors-in-chief (an editorial transition occurred during that period), going through two rounds of hefty reworkings of the ideas discussed, to the great benefit of our essay. Everyone was pleased. Things were proceeding smoothly. And it was everyone's understanding that we were moving toward publication; all that was pending was for us to add an acknowledgments section and some material responding to the latest feedback.

In July 2022, we sent in what we thought was our final draft. Our acknowledgments included an explicit note welcoming queer and trans subjects *into* psychoanalysis, as patients but also as colleagues, teachers, and analysts, and we added new paragraphs addressing issues sparked by the last round of feedback.

And then everything changed.

The journal's communications with us took a sharp turn in content and tone. We were "kindly" asked to selectively remove the lines deemed too "political" in our acknowledgments, as well as the final additions to the main text.[2] We asked why. We got no response. We protested. We were informed that publication was no

[2]   Here is the text for our acknowledgments, with the parts we were asked to remove highlighted by the *IJP*:

We want to thank the Sexual and Gender Diversity Studies Committee of the IPA for their path-clearing work overall, for their creation of the Tiresias Paper Award, and for their sturdy advocacy for an expanded psychoanalytic project. This project insists on welcoming "queer" subjects (patients as well as candidates and analysts) who have too often been treated as problems *for* psychoanalysts rather than as offering opportunities from which to think our metapsychology anew. Wresting such space is not easy nor always pleasant, but it is necessary and *critical to psychoanalysis' survival*. As such, we are honored to have received the first Tiresias Paper Award and pleased that it is appearing in the pages of the *International Journal of Psychoanalysis*. We are especially grateful to Marco Posadas, the first president of the SGDS Committee, whose fierce commitment and imagination humbles and inspires us. May future generations of queer and trans analysts and patients never encounter what many of us who are queer-identified have had to: that, more than anything, is the vision of our work in this paper.

longer a given but was now newly contingent on our compliance. We objected to this retraction of the journal's previous publication offers. Naming the repressive force did not go well; we (and the S&GDSC) received emails with legal-sounding language, including words like *slander* and *calumny*. We understood there were concerns about a possible lawsuit on account of our protest. We obtained legal advice. While we were genuinely confused by this quickly rising intensity, we were also certain we would not edit the acknowledgements or remove what were important sections of our essay. The journal suggested that, perhaps, there should have been no revisions at all, and when we pointed out that two rounds of in-depth feedback had been offered by the journal itself, we were treated as if we were being unreasonable. It was clear we had reached an impasse. Dejected, we informed the *IJP* we would take our paper elsewhere.

And then things became stranger still.

A new email from the *IJP* in which we were copied informed the S&GDSC that if our paper appeared in another journal, the committee would be "breaching its commitments" to the *IJP*. Fears of lawsuits arose again. The forked choice now appeared to be: either the *IJP* would publish their preferred version of the paper, or there would be no publication of the first Tiresias Award paper at all. We were astonished that, in addition to withdrawing its previous publication commitments, the journal now seemed to be seeking to suppress our work overall. For weeks, we hovered between horror and disbelief. We sought legal advice again. Emails aimed at resolving the issue flew back and forth, and many meetings and conversations ensued. Friends and colleagues to whom we entrusted the situation, including journal editors of other psychoanalytic publications to whom we turned for consultation, found what was transpiring bizarre and unprecedented. We continued to refuse to "straighten out" our paper. The *IJP* definitively refused to publish it.

But, in true Foucauldian manner, where there's power, there's resistance, which is another way of saying that not all is repressive in the world of psychoanalysis.

After the *IJP* debacle, we asked ourselves: if we could dream anything for this paper, what would it be? We approached Jonathan House, editor of the Unconscious in Translation Press, to see if he would be interested in publishing it as part of a small volume in his series. He agreed and encouraged us to think freely, explicitly welcoming theorizing that he might even disagree with. He also generously offered us incisive advice and made enriching suggestions that restored our faith that the work could be published.

Hence this book.

We are proud to present our Tiresias Award essay in this volume, further developed and retitled "A Feminine Boy: Trauma as Resource for Self-Theorization." The essay is introduced by Marco Posadas, S&GDSC's inaugural chair, who contextualizes the history of the S&GDSC and committee members' vision in establishing the Tiresias Award. In chapter two, we address nonbinary gender and the use of they/them pronouns, and we offer a critique of the category of cisness. The third chapter is a reprint of Jean Laplanche's canonical essay "Gender, Sex and the *Sexual*," which is one critical foundation for our own thinking. Readers not steeped in psychoanalysis may decide to skip this more technical chapter, knowing that we explain in depth all the Laplanchean ideas necessary to follow our arguments. The book concludes with a brief epilogue that is a call out to the future.

HOW WE WORK IN THIS BOOK

BOTH OF OUR ESSAYS IN this volume draw on Laplanche's groundbreaking framework vis-à-vis gender. But our writing is also heavily inflected by our engagement with trans of color critique, trans studies, Black feminism, and queer theory, as well as our own clinical experience. To put these alongside Laplanchean theory, we have not only had to use but also to stretch Laplanche's thinking.[3] His

[3]   Laplanche's thinking offers truly groundbreaking contributions to metapsychology, rewriting the very foundations of psychoanalytic thinking. As will be clear in this book, we find his ideas very helpful in pushing psychoanalysis vis-à-vis queerness and transness. But, as the reader will also discover in Appendices I and II of "Gender, Sex and the *Sexual*" (reprinted in this volume), he is not exempt from some of the problematic language and thinking about transness and race that have historically weighed down psychoanalysis.

thinking, although extraordinarily capacious, can at times lean conservative. We have thus employed this mélange of critical and clinical resources to orient ourselves toward thinking queer and trans identities' derivation—and about the ethics of doing such thinking at all.

A bit, then, about our method. In our view, putting psychoanalysis in contact with other disciplines is not a straightforward matter, nor is it simply about "enriching" psychoanalysis. Such contact involves work far more complex than merely importing new thinking *into* our field; too commonly, importing novel ideas into psychoanalysis is akin to sentencing them to a slow, invisible death, because the immediate impulse is to make incoming ideas "psychoanalytic" or to "apply" them to the clinic. Such a move, frequent and reflexive, inevitably strips such ideas of elements that are foreign to analytic theorizing, when, we argue, such foreign-ness is precisely what makes them most vitalizing *for* psychoanalysis. Much like the Minotaur, the mythological monster who is not sacrificed as ordained but is kept alive by a constant stream of youths sent to him for his consumption, psychoanalysis is kept alive in part by metabolizing the tributes of interdisciplinary contact, by appropriating them *into* its organism, effectively cannibalizing them to stay alive. Such appropriation gives the patina of interdisciplinary engagement, but it is not a sincere reckoning, as its investments lie in preserving the field's structural stability. If psychoanalysis is to survive and thrive, we maintain, it will have to be in actual contact with ideas outside its domain.

Such contact, however, is not about harmonious relations or the forging of strong, allied bonds. Psychoanalysis will need to let itself be screwed, and even to find pleasure in how it can get screwed up by such contact, so that it may become screwed differently, re-screwed through this encounter with other disciplinary domains. Part of what we present in this book is an unscrewing/rescrewing of psychoanalysis that, rather than reproducing itself, tends to the pleasures that accompany theoretical transformation. *We need, and should accept, nothing less than theoretical transformation to be able to work productively with queer and trans life.*

We are obviously not arguing for a killing of psychoanalysis overall; we firmly believe that psychoanalysis has much to offer queer and trans thinking that other thinking does not. What our Minotaur metaphor aims to convey is that those aspects of psychoanalytic theory that do not work (and many don't in the domain of gender and sexuality) cannot be kept on life support by brief injections of ideas from other fields, so that we may *look* as if we are still current even as, all the while, our institutions continue to work in ways that may well prove deadly to the field and *actively dangerous* to queer and trans life and lives. Our own experience with the *IJP* is an object lesson in such deadening.[4] What we are interested

---

[4] The fact that the journal did not stop at withdrawing their previous

in, and want to urge the reader to become curious about as well, is contact with other disciplines that is analytic *in process*, and that permits alien ideas to have lytic effects on what psychoanalysis is and might become. We are not interested in how ideas from other domains can get "used" in psychoanalytic thought, but in the perturbations such contact brings to the psychoanalytic edifice itself, in what it can help *dis-integrate*. Weathering these disturbances so that we may theorize again, and theorize better, can nudge us into rewriting some of the protocols by which we think and work with and alongside queer and trans patients and colleagues.[5]

In this spirit, throughout this volume, we focus on interdisciplinary thinking whose alien-ness to psychoanalysis operates like "a thorn in the flesh of the ego" (Laplanche 1999, 129). We encourage psychoanalysis

acceptance, but even applied pressure on the S&GDSC to ensure that our paper did not appear *anywhere* in print, suggests to us a sort of panic in response to the expansion of the psychoanalytic project overall.

[5]   We are reminded, for example, of a recent analytic conference focusing on a clinical essay written by a trans-identified colleague (Hansbury, 2017a), and the range of problematic statements made about how his transness was overstimulating to the patient and thus responsible for the patient's acting out. While indeed the analytic endeavor needs to protect the space for the range of affective responses patients may have, including transphobic ones, protecting the space *for psychoanalysts* to express transphobic ideas with conviction is neither proper nor ethical. Not only would such collusion with the patient stall the treatment; it also makes psychoanalytic institutions hostile to, and damaging of, our trans students, colleagues, supervisors, and teachers.

to welcome that impact, and we urge analysts to make it our task—*and to see it as our responsibility*—both to celebrate what these thorns do to established analytic ideas and to welcome the opportunity that this opens up *for* our metapsychology. Psychoanalysis, we believe, cannot afford to rely on "its own immediacy" or on "knowledge that borrows from nothing but itself, [knowledge] that is self-reliant, [and that is] based only on its own practice" (Laplanche 1987, 63).

WHAT WE WANT THIS BOOK TO DO

FOR A LONG TIME, WE have been preoccupied with an experience that one of us (A.P.) had with a lesbian-identified student in an undergraduate classroom.[6]

The course, taught in the late 1990s, was "Introduction to Lesbian and Gay Studies"—what might today be offered under the expanded name "Introduction to LGBTQ Studies." The tilt of the class was social constructionist, and I (A.P.) had just finished a multiday series of lectures on *The Will to Knowledge* (1976), the first volume of Michel Foucault's *History of Sexuality*. I paused for questions and comments. A lesbian student's hand shot up; in retrospect, it was more like a fist in the air. "I get it, I get it," the

---

[6]   A trained psychoanalyst, Ann Pellegrini is also a full-time faculty member at New York University, teaching classes on queer theory and psychoanalysis, religion and sexuality, and gender and performance, among other topics.

student said, somewhat impatiently. "Heterosexuality and homosexuality are socially constructed and recent historical inventions. Fine. But what I want to know is what made *me* a lesbian." The arm came down, but the challenge hung in the room. I remember saying something like this: "You're right—prior to the late nineteenth and early twentieth centuries, you might not have been able to think of yourself as a lesbian, but that still cannot tell us why *that* category, and not some other one that is also available in our current moment, grabbed *you*. Why that name and not another?"

I have never forgotten this moment, nor can I stop thinking about that encounter. I have been haunted by it; it follows me in conversations with colleagues and friends; I repeat it often in my classrooms and think about it in the clinic. Between ourselves (A.P. and A.S.) as well, we have been having ongoing conversations about it for years. We include this vignette here because it so poignantly points out how master theories (and in this instance, Foucault stands in for a larger set of accounts addressing the social construction of gender and sexuality) will not necessarily help anyone to understand themselves.[7] What we see instead is a student grappling with the gap between the sorts of macrolevel narratives the class was making available and the microlevel of how these materials touched down

---

[7] Importantly, the student's question—"what made me a lesbian?"—is about how they may account for their lesbianism: what story, in other words, they might tell themselves in trying to understand it.

in an individual life's history and experience. To put this in more Laplanchean terms, we would say that the student's question bespoke a challenge and a yearning, exposing the gulf between a cultural repertory of mythosymbolic meanings and how such meanings help individuals theorize themselves.[8]

There is indeed no definitive way of accounting for why a person alights on one name rather than another, nor do we, or they, know what may shift as new names and terms and mythosymbolic possibilities arise later. A large body of work in LGBTQ studies and the history of sexuality has persuasively established that gender and sexuality have a history. Such scholarship may startle us because it shows us just how recent we all are (Foucault 1988, 156), by demonstrating that the categories used to think, know, and organize the self are historically novel, culturally contingent formations. Perhaps this puts in a different context the current panic about nonbinary genders being an "artifact" of social changes; our sense of ourselves is not ontological, but *always an artifact*, sewn together with materials foreign to the self and scavenged from the cultural field. All gender and all sexuality, we argue in this volume, are historically contingent, where history provides

---

[8] The idea of the mythosymbolic is explicated in depth in our first chapter. For now, briefly, it is the term Laplanche (1987) gives to the set of myths, symbols, and stories that circulate in the social surround and on which human beings draw to translate *enigma,* a decentered process that yields self-theorizations that come to constitute the ego itself.

the mythosymbolic funnels through which human beings narrativize themselves. But these still don't do much to tell us about the ins and outs and idiosyncrasies of any one individual life. For this, psychoanalysis is absolutely necessary.

Interestingly, the student mentioned above now identifies as trans rather than lesbian. Considered in retrospect, this makes the question "why am I a lesbian?" possible to read differently. Might it have had to do with an emerging sense of their transness? Was this a question addressed not just to their teacher, but to themselves? Perhaps yes, perhaps no. Gender-affirmative psychoanalytic models would easily line up with such an explanatory framework. This is where our book intervenes. "Why am I a lesbian?" (and all other questions of this sort regarding the subject's own gender or sexuality[9]) shows how the process of trying to theorize oneself is always allo-centric; it proceeds not around some truth at the epicenter of the self, but is always already decentered, having to do with how subjects respond to the other's intrusive impact on us.[10] Rather than liberate an interior truth, a sense of one's

---

[9] We refer to questions asked by the subject in the process of their own self-theorization, not those asked by the analyst (or by doctors, legislators, policy makers, etc.) trying to ascertain if the patient's gender identification is "believable" or not.

[10] *Intrusion* here does not invoke some malignant invasive other who encroaches upon us (as in a violating parent or an abusive legal system), but is meant in the psychoanalytic sense where the infant is intruded upon by the adult to whom she is in an inevitable relation of asymmetry. Such asymmetries repeat throughout one's lifespan, most

identity (gendered and otherwise) arises as an outcome of the effort to organize (to bind) the surplus energy (in Laplanchean language, the enigmatic surplus) we are exposed to in the asymmetrical relation with the other.[11]

To put this more bluntly, we find the notion of *core gender identity* at best simplistic and at worst problematic. The idea that anyone is, at core, straight or gay or bi, cis or trans or nonbinary or insert-your-gender-term-here, reasserts a kind of Ptolemaic cosmology of gender and sexuality in which the true self is the centered core around which a sun of meanings rotates. We posit that anything that characterizes our sense of self precipitates through how we "treat" the other's incursion into us; the self is thus what gets "crafted" in the wake of, and in the effort to "treat," that invasiveness. At stake is not essence—for example, was A.P.'s student *really* lesbian or *really* trans— but how the subject is self-theorized at any one particular moment; this opens up space for the possibility that the student may have been lesbian then and *become* trans later.

Obviously, it is also possible that this student was trans and suppressing it all along; it is easy to imagine it may have taken time for them to come to realize their transness, to come out to others about it, and so on. We do not dispute

poignantly so in the consulting room.
[11] Laplanche's founding example of this asymmetry is the relation of the *infans* to the adult caregiver. The analytic encounter is orchestrated to re-create this asymmetry. The classroom, with its asymmetries between teacher and student, may be another engine for enigma.

this possibility and have seen many such examples in our clinical encounters. We want to offer, however, a way of thinking that permits analysts to work with ideas that have to do with the subject's development, with family history, and with intergenerational factors, which may become elements through which the subject improvises ("translates," in Laplanchean terminology) their gender.[12] To situate gender in the domain of translation is to say that there is nothing authentic about one's gender *other than one's experience of it.* And it is also to sign up for gender as a wildly improvisational process, which is not rooted in any "observable" or "objective" fact (e.g., body morphology or chromosomes), nor in any imaginary interiorized idea (e.g., core gender identity). What this means is that gender cannot be confirmed or disconfirmed: it *simply exists* in relation to how it is experienced at the moment.

It is easy to see the dangers posed by taking gender and sexuality seriously in the way we are proposing. If trans or queer experience cannot be codified into anything outside experience, and if gender is something both out of our willful control, but also deeply personal and connected to the subject's autonomous self-theorizations,[13] what else of

---

[12] In chapter one, we explain Laplanche's model of gender so that readers unfamiliar with his work can fully engage our argument. We hope that this will also serve as a handy orientation to the third chapter of this volume, a republication of Laplanche's "Gender, Sex and the *Sexual.*"

[13] Autonomy here does not imply conscious agency, but a freedom from being forced to translate in any one singular way. Such prohibition to

what we understand as reality could give way? What will such thinking do to race or to religion? Our first chapter examines these issues in magnification. We will see there how critical it is that we give up the nonsensical idea that trans or genderqueer people have different psychological wiring, or that a particular set of hormonal or genetic factors may one day be discovered that will account for those differences. If we can give up on teaching our candidates stupidities about how some people are just trans whereas others are just cis, born this way, if we can resist the fiction that there's something bedrock about trans- or any other gender-conventional or gender-expansive experience for that matter, psychoanalysis has a chance of discussing more openly *and with less shame* that gender, *all gender,* is both delightfully stranger *and* more savagely violent than our theories can imagine.

What facile ideas about gender diversity being genetic or anchored in some inner core do is diminish the strange agency that *becoming* trans, *becoming* nonbinary, and *becoming* queer entails. In chapter one, we describe this agency as *strange*—and elaborate on what makes it unusual, and why we see it as related to the subject's autonomy—to highlight that we are not speaking of agency in the neoliberal sense, as if subjects were free to

translate freely, "intromission" in Laplanche's terms, is traumatic on the level of the psyche, but is not necessarily experienced as painful or traumatic. It therefore requires much layered analytic work in order to be uncovered and brought to the analytic dyad's attention.

"select" how they will translate their gender. We provide a framework that refuses "born this way" notions of queer and trans experience in order to show that what gives gender its intrapsychic grip is the fact that it proceeds from the subject's own auto-poietic process: it is this that makes one's gender feel one's own even as it is stitched from materials that are not of one's own creation.[14] What this highly mobile process also means is that that we do not (and cannot) control our own or another's gender-becoming. If gender is a translation, as this volume presumes, then it is neither a volitional outcome nor a process that can be steered by an other.

To account for gender this way is to look at development not as an "unfold[ing] of isolated potentials" nor as a "succession of steps or stages" (Laplanche 1987, 66) within a teleology, but as a sequence of external and psychic events that may be seen as a developmental path towards an outcome only in retrospect. The "how" and "where to" of gender formation, in other words, can only be considered in the rearview mirror. Remember Freud who, in "Psychogenesis of a Case of Homosexuality in a Woman" (1922), tries to sort out whether he can explain *why* his patient is a lesbian; reading this paper is to watch him stumble across the page in muddled confusion. Amidst his chaotic thinking, though, at a particularly

---

[14] We borrow the term *autopoiesis* from the writings of Dominique Scarfone (2021); this composite term comes from the Greek words εαυτός, "self," and ποίησις, "production."

lucid moment, he writes:

> So long as we trace the development from its final
> outcome backwards, the chain of events appears
> continuous, and we feel we have gained an insight
> which is completely satisfactory or even exhaustive.
> But if we proceed the reverse way, if we start from
> the premises inferred from the analysis and try to
> follow these up to the final result, then we no longer
> get the impression of an inevitable sequence of events
> which could have been otherwise determined. We
> notice at once that there might have been another
> result, and that we might have been just as well able
> to understand and explain the latter. The synthesis is
> thus not so satisfactory as the analysis; in other words,
> from a knowledge of the premises we could not have
> foretold the nature of the result. (Freud 1922, 167)

His idea—that sexual and gender formations cannot
be predicted "along the lines of synthesis" (1922, 168),
but that accounting for them always involves the work
of retrospection—reminds us that translations are
understandable only retrospectively, oftentimes a blend
of accident and improvisation. Freud implies that what in
real time looks like data points on a scatter block, without
a single discernible trend, can look like breadcrumbs on
a trail when viewed in rearview and after the outcome is
known.

Freud's point is to highlight that this synthesis can
only happen after the fact; it cannot be predicted ahead
of time. And yet, Laplanche would counter, even this

retroactive recasting of scattered data points into putative breadcrumbs is not a developmental arc that becomes clear only after the fact. Any such developmental account, he emphasizes, is itself an ex-post-facto construction, more the product of the conditions under which that synthesis happens than an accurate, true rendering of the process itself (1987).

Wait, you may reasonably object: developmental events matter; they are not constructions or fantasies. And in fact, Laplanche would agree with that. But what matters even more, he would point out, is not the "emergence" of this history (as if its meaning is fixed or settled ahead of time), but the situating of these events "in relation to the conditions that make [their emergence] possible" (1987, 67). To say it differently, this kind of retrospective accounting may feel to the analyst as if they were finally able to figure out the developmental factors that really mattered in the subject's becoming—turning some data points into breadcrumbs while revealing the rest as mere points in the scatter plot. However, any such formation is but one way of putting them together to tell a coherent story. So yes, these data points may be factually true, nor can "psychoanalysis avoid referring to a history" (69), but the psychoanalytic specificity of this process has to do with the unconscious and with sexuality.

What does sexuality have to do with this, you may ask? As we'll see in chapter one, it has to do with the very laying down of these data points *by others*, a process that implicates the adult's sexual unconscious. This means that the path of gender-becoming is always related to the droppings of others who preceded us: the others of family and of culture. Some of these droppings, we propose, may have to do with trauma.

HOW TO WORK AS AN ANALYST: THE RESOURCE OF COMPLEXITY

THIS BOOK IS NOT A technical manual, even as it has strong recommendations to make.

What it offers instead is an exploration of how gender and sexual experience accrues out of processes of self-theorization (translation, but also de-translation and re-translation), which have more to do with felt experience than with truth or with authenticity (Salamon, 2010). Our second chapter is dedicated to what we think of as the analyst taking sides, though not with a particular translation (translations come undone and get redone in the course of an analysis), but siding with the patient's translational freedom.[15] Our stance accords with what we understand Marquis Bey to be saying when they discuss the distinction between being an accomplice and an ally (2021). An accomplice, for us, is not someone who thoughtlessly charges on, someone who mindlessly supports and validates, or a person who contributes to the

---

[15]   Again, this is not the freedom of (neo)liberal choice, but the freedom from prohibition, including the analyst's no.

patient's self-theorization. Unlike an ally, the analyst as an accomplice dirties their hands, claws at theory that is tainted, gets "in and get[s] sullied by the struggle" (2021, 223) of dissolving analytic theorizing about gender that has its foothold in some notion of internal "truth."

But if gender is not about some ontologically true interiority, what, you might reasonably wonder, *is* it about, and how do we work with it in the consulting room?

This is where our book intervenes in current conversations about gender both within and without psychoanalysis to strongly advocate for thinking about gender as having a history of becoming. Being able to formulate clinical hypotheses about how someone's gender came into being can invoke processes that, in the consulting room, may support the flourishing of atypically gendered patients. We insist on this because we believe that eliminating transphobia in the field is a necessary *but starkly insufficient* condition for working well with queer and trans patients; what is required is nothing less than being able to join patients in their explorations of their genders, *without resisting the inventiveness gender necessarily involves*. This is an exploration, we hasten to add, that follows the patient's timeline, not the analyst's.

The resource of such complexity and nuance is routinely available to and utilized by analysts in work with normatively gendered patients. Think, for example, of Little Hans, the young boy treated by Freud (1909), whose entire case study is dedicated to thinking about the constitution of his boyhood. The theorizing of how normative gender comes about, in other words, is neither unheard of (as many of us have mistakenly thought) nor is it rare: psychoanalysis has always been thinking about the gender formation of cis people; *but it has not been doing so with an eye toward changing the patient's gender.* And such theorizing has, in fact, proved extremely helpful—for example, when a colleague writes about probing a (cis?) woman's femininity (her feminine identifications and counteridentifications, defenses around masculine wishes, anxieties and rigidities about what is feminine or not, etc.) in order to help her de-tangle her gender experience from parental or societal gender expectations, or to help her decide for herself if she wants to have children, or how aggressive she can be in negotiating a promotion, or in advocating for herself in a relationship.

What we want to underline is this: our professional literature is *rife* with examples of analysts working with normatively gendered patients—tracking aspects of their gender formation to expand psychic capacities, to diminish shame, to imagine wider potentialities, to build and sustain better relationships, to expand pleasure, and so on. Take, for instance, Jessica Benjamin's work where she elucidates how some women's femininities can be seen as a way of coping with paternal absence (1991), thus opening up space for more emancipated forms of feminist living; or Muriel Dimen's writings, which powerfully show how fears of dependency issuing from conflicted maternal identifications can inflect a woman's sense of her independence or desirability (1991, 2005), such that addressing these can enable her to want and strive bigger; or Dianne Elise's robust theoretical framework that shows how male fears of psychic penetration amount to hardened psychic surfaces (2001), and how addressing these in the transference can soften the grasp of toxic masculinity. We mention this sampling of analysts who do complex work with normative genders to show that *thinking around gender complexity that does not seek to change the patient's gender, but instead uses its constitution to deepen a treatment, is neither an exception nor a novelty in the psychoanalytic tradition.* To the contrary, this is a tested, established, and valued way of working *that is not extended to atypically gendered patients.*

"Cis-folks," writes Hil Malatino, "get to be understood as affectively complex and ambivalent in relation to all sorts of phenomena…[including their] gender….Why not trans people?" (2022, 3). It is in this spirit, that of wanting to offer conceptual frameworks by which this resource might be made available to sexual and gender minoritized patients, that we offer our theorizing in this book.

The risk remains, of course, that fleshing out ideas about the constitution of gender atypicalities will be weaponized, used against such minoritarian patients to serve oppressive conversion goals—in short, that it will be put to work in virulently transphobic clinical practices or used to advocate conversion therapies. We worry about such misuse and have had multiple, hours-long conversations about it with colleagues whose values and commitment to queer and trans life we trust. Even as we worry about such misuse, however, we have come to believe that this risk is a fact that simply needs to be accepted. We cannot guard against every possible misunderstanding or misuse of our work. Moreover, what if such risk is in fact inevitable whenever new ideas arise, ideas that argue for a sharp turn in a discipline's thinking? We do not ask this question nonchalantly, as if we didn't care about the possibility that our ideas may be abused in a way that could cause harm, but because we believe that it is ethically necessary, urgent even, to refuse the pressure to offer oversimplified narratives and to engage instead in a more searching conversation, without being inhibited by the fear that anything complex or nuanced will be put to violent use.

To be explicit, then: *there is nothing wrong with being gay, lesbian, queer, gender nonconforming, or trans, nor is any of these an undesirable or pathological outcome*. Genderqueer and sexually diverse individuals can and do live full, pleasurable, exciting lives—which is not to say that they are spared the miseries that befall everyone as part of the human condition. Indeed, trans people and queer people should get to have *all* the feels, including negative or bad feelings (Amin 2023; Chu 2018; Malatino 2022).

Trans people are often in a double bind when it comes to misery. As Kadji Amin explains (2023), medicopsychological models of transness posit "negative affect…in the form of gender dysphoria" as a definitional symptom of transness. As a result, "[i]n many national contexts, feeling bad is a diagnostic requirement to access transition-related care" (33). But making misery—dysphoria—into the symptom that transition is supposed to fix may create the mistaken expectation, let alone the impossible demand, that transition will forever banish all unhappy feelings (Amin 2023; Chu 2018). There are, Amin pointedly underlines, many reasons why trans unhappiness may persist on the other side of transition, but not due to some ontology of transness. The medical model cannot comprehend the social determinants of "trans people's distress," among them: "Racism, transphobia, hypervisibility, social isolation, lack of access to health care, imprisonment, the fallout of self-protective coping mechanisms, and even the way that passing renders transness shameful and secretive" (2023, 37). Negative affect and trans negativity are not only "ordinary for trans folk," but are often an "integral part of a trans affective commons" (Malatino 2022, 4-5). Importantly, and as we will argue in connection with the clinical material in chapter one, the negative affect of trauma may be not a symptom of trauma, but part of its generative source material.

No doubt the presumed "wrongness" of gender diversity continues to be a powerful current in the psychoanalytic world.[16] For example, as recently as 2021, prominent

---

[16] As we discuss in the first chapter, this presumption underlies

analysts discussed in the pages of the *IJP* the following question: "Would you hope, would you feel—yes, I look forward to my grandchild becoming transgender?" (Blass and Bell, in Blass, Bell, and Saketopoulou 2021, 984). This question, as Saketopoulou underscored in the same exchange, is presented as if it implies its own answer: of course, no one would *want* their hypothetical grandchild to be trans, because actual trans children are to be understood as de facto unwanted, *and all sound analysts would recognize that as a fact.* This attitude is chilling.[17] We mean this doubly: it is chilling to see professionals speak about transness as a terrible fate that no one would want for their child and to do so shamelessly and without compunction or editorial intervention *in print*; and also, this hostility to gender and sexual diversity is so often unambiguous, unambivalent, and unequivocal that it chills any impulse to theorize away from born-this-way arguments.

But it is vital not to accede to this blackmail. *Gender Without Idenity* offers solid psychoanalytic thinking to

"gender exploratory therapies," which may themselves be mutations of conversion practices (see Ashley 2022).

[17] It is important for analysts to understand that this violence against children has a long and sad lineage in analytic history. In recently published material from the archive of psychoanalyst Robert Stoller (who is responsible for coining the term *core gender identity*), the description of a therapy session with a five-year-old child concludes with the following words: "I would not want him for my son" (quoted in Gill-Peterson 2018, 150).

contest traumatophobic[18] stances that reflexively assume that if trauma has a share in the development of atypical genders and non-normative sexualities, that necessarily delegitimizes them. Pushing back against the way that traumatophobic logics see anything that is connected with trauma as cause for suspicion or alarm, we advocate for thinking about trauma not to question the validity of trans and queer life, but to articulate its textures.

We propose this theorizing, then, because we believe that psychoanalysis can no longer afford to let homotransphobic[19] panics constrain what we can and cannot say, especially in print, for fear that our words will be used against queer and trans existence. It is time to start telling more complex stories about atypical genders and sexualities, and to engage in more sophisticated theorizing around their becoming. We wrote this book in this spirit: not as an uber-theory of atypical gender constitution,

---

[18] The term *traumatophobia*, sourced from Saketopoulou's work (2023a, 2023b), refers to the rigid ways in which trauma is seen in analytic life as creating damage or catastrophe, making it hard to remain attuned to the ways in which it sets in motion energies that can be taken up in positively transformative ways.

[19] We offer the composite term *homotransphobia* to serve one of this book's arguments: that phobias generated by transness (and gender expansiveness more generally) and those generated by homosexuality are not distinct, but rather entangled moral panics. Consider, for example, how some opposition to gender-affirmative care for trans youth justifies itself on the grounds that these trans youth are "really" gay kids whose desire to transition symptomatizes internalized homophobia. This kind of thinking effectively pits sexuality against gender when gender and sexuality are, in fact, always entwined.

but as proof that it is possible to look in the rearview developmental mirror to consider paths for how atypical genders may have been formed without insinuating a detour from a "normal" gender course—and without such theorizing thereby capsizing into conversion therapy. We can't emphasize enough, however, that those paths are not, as already discussed, developmental truths, but are themselves conditioned by the circumstances of their emergence (i.e., how they are synthesized, by whom, and under what conditions in the analysis).

We are thus not moving to prescribe how any gay, queer, or trans subject would tell the story of their own origin (Sedgwick 1990), as if we were issuing a ban on born-this-way or "true self" self-narrativizations. Such a ban would contradict how we see psychoanalytic ethics: namely, that individuals do their own self-theorizing, engaging in their own auto-poietic projects. Our interest is rather in making room for more ways *for psychoanalysts* to understand gender and sexuality's evolutions. Only when the self-accounts of our patients command the analyst's genuine respect can space open up for both patient and analyst to become interested in their psychic meanings. Curiosity, however, should not be misused in some furtive way as a path to eliminating difference, nor as an alibi to prevent transitioning but as a way of supporting the patient's growth and flourishing. It is this—*queer and trans people's growth and flourishing*—that is at the beating heart of the volume you have begun to read.

Introduction to Chapter 1
THE STAFF OF TIRESIAS: RESISTANCE, REVOLT, RUPTURES, AND REPAIRING IN PSYCHOANALYSIS TODAY[1]
Marco Posadas[2]

I WANT TO TAKE THIS opportunity to share some of my experiences of being the inaugural chair of the Sexual and Gender Diversity Studies Committee (S&GDSC) to provide context for the first International Psychoanalytical Association (IPA) Tiresias Paper Award. This award was part of the mandate that also created the S&GDSC of the IPA during Stefano Bolognini's administration in 2017. The committee was supported by Virginia Ungar and Sergio Nick, as well as Andrew Brook's administration, and it continues today with the support of Harriet Wolfe, Adriana Prengler, and Henk Delawyk and under the

---

[1] In the original plan, in which the Tiresias essay would have appeared in the *IJP*, the winning essay would have been preceded by an essay by Marco Posadas, the S&GDSC inaugural chair, to contextualize the newly established award and the committee's role in the IPA. Without an *IJP* publication, these important framings would also have been lost. We thus include this essay *Gender Without Identity* not as an introduction to our paper per se, but to give the committee's work and the award's intent a home alongside the first Tiresias publication.

[2] Marco Posadas, Ph.D., MSW, RSW, FIPA is a psychoanalyst, clinical social worker, and licensed psychologist (MEX). He maintains a clinical practice in Toronto. He was recipient of the 2013 Ontario Association of Social Workers Inspirational Leader Award and named the 2022 Social Worker of the Year in Toronto for his work with underserved and marginalized populations.

leadership of Leticia Glocer Fiorini, who succeeded me as chair.

The S&GDSC was envisioned and proposed in 2014 by an interregional task force; since its conception, the resistance that the topic of sexuality in general, and gender diversity in particular, has occasioned in psychoanalysis has been loud and clear. Before the first task force was approved by the IPA Board, it was public knowledge that the board at that time did not see the need for such a committee. That tone of misunderstanding has persisted. One consistent concern discussed in the early task force, and later on during my tenure as inaugural chair of the S&GDSC, was how to manage the resistances that we anticipated coming up in the membership when psychoanalysis moves from thinking about gender as a binary to gender as a polymorphic phenomenon. What types of resistances will be faced? This has been particularly important as the committee has attempted to carry out our mandate to carve out a space to be able to discuss in a scientific, respectful, and amicable way the complex topic of sexual and gender diversities, and to contribute from a psychoanalytic perspective. That the first paper to receive the Tiresias Award is being published in the book you are now reading shows how hard-won such spaces continue to be and the ongoing struggle for a queer and trans psychoanalysis.

As the S&GDSC identified the gap between psychoanalytic contributions to the field of gender diversity and sexualities, and contributions from gender studies, lesbian and gay studies, queer studies, sociology, anthropology, psychology, etc., we realized the need for a strategic plan in each region. Each region has a co-chair; during the first term of the S&GDSC, the co-chairs were Frances Thomson-Salo (Europe), Victor Bonfilio (North America), and Leticia Glocer Fiorini (Latin America), and they coordinated regional subcommittees, each comprised of three members (including an IPSO representative) and four consultants. It was the second largest committee of the IPA after the board of directors, and its establishment elicited noticeable curiosity and questions about how we would be able to carry out our mandate. These remain live questions.

The impact of the IPA's status as a world organization can be seen in the wide diversity of perspectives when it comes to our understandings of and contributions to the emotional well-being and mental health of patients who identify as members of LGBTQ+ communities. The committee's challenge has been to bridge the gap between the contributions of institutionalized psychoanalysis and the contemporary trends arising at the intersection of psychoanalysis and gender and sexual diversities. The IPA Tiresias Award became the platform to highlight the type of psychoanalytic contributions that we hope can strengthen and deepen psychoanalysts' understandings and formulations about working clinically with these communities of people.

The chapter you are about to read by Dr. Avgi Saketopoulou and Dr. Ann Pellegrini is an example of the type of contributions the committee wants to recognize and promote. A shorter version of it—under the title "A Feminine Boy: Normative Investments and Reparative Fantasy at the Intersections of Gender, Race, and Religion"—was awarded the first Tiresias Paper Award, in 2021. Their work helpfully brings together institutionalized psychoanalysis and academic contributions at the intersection of gender and sexual diversity.

As is usually the case in psychoanalysis, historical narratives, metaphors, and myths have supported our thinking and theorizing. In this case, it was the Greco-Roman myth of Tiresias, one of the few figures in mythology who illustrates an archaic idea of gender transition. The Tiresias myth in general, and specifically the moment when Tiresias stops a violent reaction in the face of something ambiguous and undecipherable, has become of particular importance for understanding the type of resistances that S&GDSC members have been facing while doing this work. This moment in the Tiresias myth represents a change in the history of violence against vulnerable and marginalized aspects of the human experience, serving as inspiration for the committee's logo and award.

S E X U A L
A N D
G E N D E R
D I V E R S I T Y
S T U D I E S
C O M M I T T E E

THE MYTH OF TIRESIAS

THE MYTH OF TIRESIAS IS not a universal model for trans representation, nor is it a trans allegory. This myth has been previously used in psychoanalytic writing to convey an alternative to restrictive and heteronormative models of thinking gender and sexuality, such as the Oedipus complex (Cavanagh 2016, 2018), and to better understand analytic listening and interpretation (Webb, Bushnell, and Widseth 1993). The emphasis is usually on Tiresias as the oracle who foresaw Oedipus's future, omitting other aspects of the myth that can stimulate thinking about how to face violent reactions to gender polymorphism in the clinical situation and in institutionalized psychoanalysis (e.g., in training and knowledge creation and exchange).

As a cornerstone of the IPA Tiresias Award, I would like to focus on the violent response of Tiresias in the face of something ambiguous and unintelligible (Brisson 2002), and on the alternative of not acting violently when confronting something we do not understand. How can we develop a way of psychoanalytic thinking that helps us understand our intense reactions when we encounter gender polymorphism?

Psychoanalytic knowledge has historically relied on Greco-Roman mythology as a set of narratives that can enrich our thinking about conscious and unconscious dynamics. The myth of Tiresias (as retold by Ovid in Brisson 2002) can serve as a tool with which to make enigmatic (Laplanche 2007) and ambiguous aspects of gender (Gherovici 2010, 2017; Gill-Peterson 2018; Glocer Fiorini 2015; Gozlan 2008, 2014) accessible to psychoanalysts and psychoanalytic candidates. It serves as a scaffolding to help us understand a type of enactment whereby aspects of gender difference are experienced as systematically influencing the mind of the clinician.

There are several versions of the myth of Tiresias, some contradicting each other. Tiresias is the "official diviner of the royal house of Thebes" (Brisson 2002, 123), and he is one of the few—and probably the most important— trans characters in Greco-Roman mythology. He goes from being a man to living as a woman for seven years/ generations, and is then transformed into a man again.

Tiresias's story begins with his walking with the aid of a staff that was gifted to him by Apollo, the god of light, healing, and the sun (among other things). Tiresias encounters something undecipherable and undistinguishable at Mount Cyllene: two snakes tightly coiled together while copulating. According to one version of the story, the sight of copulating snakes offends Tiresias, and he uses the staff to hit the female snake, thereby wounding her. This deed triggers the rage of the goddess Hera, wife of Zeus, king of the gods, who transforms Tiresias into a woman as punishment for wounding the vulnerable female snake. Tiresias, now female, goes on to marry, have children, practice religion, and grow old—all thought to be culturally appropriate female roles in antiquity (Brisson 2002).

It is useful to consider that Apollo's staff, used as a support for walking, can represent male privilege and male-perpetrated violence, as well as the supportive and claustrophobic functions of gender policing that can be derivatives of the superego. Apollo's staff can also be a symbolic representation of the white Phallus, where violence is used in the name of the law. A personal goal of mine as a psychoanalyst working with LGBTQ+ populations—and working within psychoanalysis, as well, to create venues for advancing psychoanalytic thinking about LGBTQ+ issues (as in the Tiresias Award)—is to address and end the violence perpetrated against these communities. In the Tiresias myth, gender and sexual ambiguity cause offense when encountered unexpectedly.

But this is not ancient history. Research shows that trans and gender-expansive people are often the target of violence, usually perpetrated by white cisgender heterosexual males. The gay and trans panic defenses frequently used in court to justify violence against trans women of color resonate with the violent response to gender and sexual ambiguity seen in the Tiresias myth. The feminine, represented as the vulnerable other(ed) sex, can serve as a form of punishment for perceived male-centered gender transgressions.

This can be found in the first formulation of gender transitioning as a psychotic idea in Freud's formulation of Schreber's case, in which he dismisses Schreber's narcissistic delusional core, despite all the symptomatology: "The idea of being transformed into a woman was the salient feature and the earliest germ of his delusional system" (1911, 21). This unfortunate Freudian misstep caused the transitional quality of gendered experiences to wrongfully became the foundation for core delusional systems.

Seven years later (or seven generations later, depending on the version of the myth), Tiresias, now a woman, again finds two snakes copulating. This time she follows Apollo's advice not to hit the female snake and in fact not to hit any snake, although some versions of the myth speak of Tiresias hitting the male snake instead. In any case, Hera transforms her back into a male as a reward for learning his/her lesson. Tiresias, now a male, gets in trouble again, this time at a gathering at Mount Olympus. He is summoned by Zeus to answer a question about the other sex, and his reply once again enrages Hera. Hera then gouges out Tirasias's eyes, blinding him for revealing the mysteries of women to Zeus. Zeus, feeling guilty for having asked the question that led to Hera's rage, but unable to undo another god's spell, gives Tiresias the gift of prophecy, long life, and possession of his memories even after death (Brisson 2002).

Tiresias is the diviner who foretells Oedipus's destiny, and he is a mediator "positioned in an intermediate state between life and death" (Brisson 2002, 126). His answer to Zeus's question—"Who feels more sexual pleasure, men or women?"—has been highlighted within queer theory, gender studies, and sociology (Brisson 2002; Cavanagh 2018). Tiresias responds that, on a scale of one to ten for sexual pleasure, with ten being the highest, women enjoy sexual pleasure at the level of nine, while men experience only a one.

The IPA Tiresias Award was conceived to focus on the moment when Tiresias encounters something ambiguous, the coiled snakes on Mount Cyllene, that provokes a violent urge to wound the female snake with his walking stick. Tiresias exemplifies one possible reaction when we encounter something at first glance undecipherable and undistinguishable, yet the myth also allows us to move away from a binary system of understanding gender and instead to carve out a space for gender polymorphism.

This His-story is missing something important: the acknowledgment of harm that institutionalized psychoanalysis has done to LGBTQ+ patients and LGBTQ+ members of the IPA. I do not think our institutions are ready to begin this process. One of the many reasons behind this book's publication is precisely the urgency of speaking out against this harm. But doing no further harm is not enough. Psychoanalysis needs to match the spirit of the Stonewall Riots of June 1969, sparked by a trans woman of color who was not going to take it any more.[3] It may be hard to believe that in this day and age, in some areas across the four regions of the IPA, competent mental health graduates are prevented from accessing training at psychoanalytic institutes due to their gender identity, ethnic background, and sometimes even their immigrant status. The first Tiresias Award has the privilege to honor two writers who have spoken out against these types of harms.

Dr. Saketopoulou and Dr. Pellegrini's work is an example of a clinical formulation that aims to decrease the violence against gender diverse patients that can happen in psychoanalytic settings. These authors show us how to slow Tiresias's blows while also helping us think about gender polymorphism and sexual diversity in the clinical setting. Simultaneously, they engage issues of race and religion. For their commitment to making the first IPA Tiresias Award a reality, I would like to thank the award's judges—Dr. Stefano Bolognini, Dr. Ken Corbett, Dr. Abel Fainstein, and Dr. Patricia Gherovici—as well as the members of the Award Subcommittee: Dr. Silvia Acosta and Dr. Leticia Glocer Fiorini.

---

[3]   We may be reminded here of another critical moment in the history of North American queer activism, the 1981 Toronto Bathhouse Raids.

1

A FEMININE BOY: TRAUMA AS RESOURCE FOR SELF-THEORIZATION

[It is crucial] to be able to let unexpected, perhaps unprecedented forms take shape within oneself, about which one will not immediately be asked to explain oneself, to give an account. Transitory forms that will make their way towards more clarity, but [which drag] behind them a shadow, advancing surrounded by a small mist of enigma through which the other, his thought, intrigues me, attracts me or repels me, it doesn't matter, but in any case makes a difference, forces me into a detour.

—Dominique Scarfone, "The Disappearance of the Shadows"

WHETHER SEEN AS AN ISSUE that sparks controversy (Blass 2020), requires dialogue (Gozlan, Osserman, Silber, Wallerstein, Watson, and Wiggins 2022), or provokes debate (Blass, Bell, and Saketopoulou 2021), queer childhood has become a central preoccupation in contemporary psychoanalysis.[1] This focus is not, as

---

[1]   Under *queer childhood,* we include trans and otherwise atypically gendered children, as well as gay children. Queer childhood encompasses both gendered and sexual non-normativities, the

many analysts seem to think, because activists within and outside psychoanalysis are pushing a "specialty" topic, nor is it because childhood queerness is now more visible in the larger social world, bringing more such patients into our consulting rooms (though increased visibility is certainly the case). If queer childhood is becoming such a heated topic, it is because it is the domain where otherwise revered psychoanalytic ideas prove unhelpful, at times even harmful. We could say, then, that like the proverbial canary in the coal mine, queer childhood forces a reckoning, as it reveals that some of psychoanalysis's foundational ideas lead both our metapsychology and our clinical praxis astray. To put it bluntly, queer childhood confronts psychoanalysis with where we have come up short. Indeed, atypical genders require us to urgently revise the role psychoanalysis has ascribed to biology in psychic life (as if biological sex were gender determinative); to rethink the libidinal alongside gender (as if gender and sexuality were wholly distinct [González 2019; Gozlan 2021]); and to become more discerning about when action should be understood as acting out (as if all action

distinctive character of which may not coagulate until later in life (or never); this reveals the futility of separating sexuality from gender. The recent tendency in progressive analytic institutes to organize training and continuing education as if gender and sexuality belong to distinctive spheres of psychic functioning is thus unfortunate, in our opinion, because it cleaves discussions about gender from eroticism and from the operations of the sexual unconscious. Imagining that the two can be parsed out creates problems both in our theory and in our consulting rooms.

in the domain of gender transition is to be conceptualized as unbridled discharge).

Instead of revisiting and revising its own foundations, psychoanalysis too easily falls into a search for origins, asking what "causes" transness, gender beyond the binary, and sexual queerness. This etiological quest to explain queer childhood has struck some analysts as just part of the ordinary purview of psychoanalysis. According to this way of proceeding, we ask "why" of all other psychic formations, so why would we exempt gender from the analyst's etiological search (Bell 2020; Blass 2020; D'Angelo, Marchiano, and Gorin 2022; Evans and Evans 2021)? Others counter that etiological quests are never neutral, because in actual practice, asking the question "why?" of non-normative sexualities or genders too often occurs in the service of illuminating their origins in order to "cure" and, effectively, eradicate them. For such critics, and we count ourselves among them, etiological quests function as stealthy starting points for the motoring of conversion therapies (Ashley 2022; Gill-Peterson 2018; Hansbury 2017b; Saketopoulou 2022; Wiggins, in Gozlan et al. 2022).

On many occasions, the conversation analysts want to have (or think we should be having) around queerness and transness is what causes it, because why, this logic goes, wouldn't we want to "fix" it? Isn't it reasonable, if not ethical, to prevent anyone from having to face the varied discriminations and difficulties that await those who live outside norms? Is it not clinically indicated to help individuals find ways to live in their assigned gender so they may be "spared" medical interventions, and the anguish of being, for example, trans (D'Angelo 2020)?

To us, etiologically and teleologically driven treatments are both cruel and dangerous. We see interventions that work toward "sparing" the patient from being trans or from "having to" transition as highly unethical and, in fact, eugenicist.[2] It is no exaggeration to point out the deadly meliorism of psychoanalytic treatments that seem more interested in eliminating transness than in helping patients live and flourish despite the real harms of discrimination trans people so often face. Gender polymorphism is not a symptom to be resolved any more than gender typicality is. Nor do analysts possess exceptional skills of prediction as to what gender a patient would best occupy. Critically, it is not our job to impose on our patients our own values as to what will or will not be a good life. Analysts with little personal contact with trans or queer individuals outside the clinic (that is, most analysts) can have an especially narrow perspective on what queer life has to offer, and may be overly influenced by panic-driven opinion pieces in the media and social anxieties around gender and sexual diversities. To presume that the analyst knows best embroils the analyst's omnipotent and omniscient fantasizing, and that needs serious countertransference analysis.[3]

---

[2] On this crucial point, see Gill-Peterson 2018.
[3] In our experience, an inability to see such a conviction as

Although we categorically reject the idea that queerness is something that the analyst should work to eliminate, we also find problematic those clinical approaches that treat non-normative gender or sexualities as fixed or as a reflection of some internal "truth," because such approaches misunderstand that *all* gender/sexuality[4] is an *unfolding and dynamic* psychic process, not a static or a predetermined one. In other words, from a psychoanalytic perspective, no gender position—be it cis, trans, nonbinary, or otherwise genderqueer—can be reasonably attributable to some "core gender identity" or seen as an expression of a "true self." All gender positions[5] (again, including cis

---

countertransference in the first place is one of the most emblematic marks of conversion therapies.

[4] In this book, phrases like *all gender* and *all sexualities,* or, more simply, *gender* and *sexuality,* reference everyone who has a gender and everyone who has a sexuality, that is, *every human being, including normatively gendered and heterosexual persons.* We stress this because it is not unusual for individuals who never give their own gender or sexuality any thought (because the world is made to accommodate them, as is the case with more typically gendered and heterosexual folks), to think that the terms do not apply to them, or to take the term *gender* as referring to *atypical gender* only. This privilege—of never having to think about your gender or sexuality as such—is also sutured to whiteness. As a body of work in Black feminist thought, queer of color critique, and trans of color critique highlights, gender and sexuality and "the meanings attached to [them]...are always and already racialized meanings" (Bey 2022, 66).

[5] We use the term *positions* to underscore that while in real time these are often experienced and lived as identities, there is no telling how stable or shifting they may be; it is only in their aftermath that we discover if such a formation is sustained, and many factors play a role in that. We want to stress, however, that if gender shifts happen, these do

male genders and cis female genders) arise out of complex psychic processes that are by no means reducible to biology alone. We will offer one way to think about these processes in what follows, drawing on the work of Jean Laplanche. But, for now, we want to stress the following: to say that gender arises through such intricate processes means that gender is something we all *acquire* and, consequently, that all genders have a constitution we can probe, examine, and theorize.

Gender constitution, in other words, extends beyond the body's sexed markers and bodily morphology and cannot be taken as the arbiter of what gender one is or will become (Salamon, 2010). Gender assignment, which is usually based on visual inspection of this bodily morphology at birth, is not a description of a truth, which the child may successfully express or from which they may later deviate, *but a set of propositional statements and practices that the child may or may not adopt.* An individual's gender, in our view, is not explicable through notions of "true gender" or "core gender identity." For this reason, while we strongly oppose the hunt for etiological factors (as if the "why" can ever be pinned down), we still advocate

not occur through an other's endeavors to change them, be that clinical intervention, relational sanction, or outright coercion. What the latter accomplish is either to make non-normative subjects hide their gender expression for fear of rejection or reprisal, or to traumatize them in a way that leads their non-normativity to go underground while they themselves become unconsciously embroiled in the suppression of their own experience (see, e.g., Schevers 2022; Urquhart 2021).

for thinking about development in a dynamic way, which is to say in a way that considers the unconscious and the sexual. More on how that stance differs from both etiology and development*alism* will follow shortly. For now, we want to emphasize that we are critical of "born-this-way" approaches to *all* genders and *all* sexualities.

THE ORIGINS AND GOALS OF "BORN-THIS-WAY" AND A CRITIQUE OF "CORE GENDER IDENTITY"

Born-this-way theorizations first appear in psychoanalytic discourse through Stoller's influential formulation of gender identity (1964, 1968). Stoller postulated a core gender identity that is intrinsic to one's sense of self, proposing this concept in an attempt to account for children who were presenting with atypical genders. Stoller's claimed investment was in explaining why these children presented in "unusual" ways, without entirely collapsing their difference into pathology.[6] But what we want to focus on at the moment is that for

---

[6] Even this story of Stoller's goals requires revision. In her carefully researched and archivally rich book, *Histories of the Transgender Child* (2018), Jules Gill-Peterson dedicates considerable space to previously unpublished quotations from Stoller's therapy sessions that illustrate the damaging practices to which he subjected the children he treated (2018). For analysts not familiar with this part of psychoanalytic history, we cannot recommend Gill-Peterson's scholarship strongly enough; it is hard and sobering reading.

Stoller, core gender identity was primarily a "biological force," which, "hidden from conscious and preconscious awareness, nonetheless seems to provide some of the drive energy for gender identity" (1964, 220). We thus see how the psychoanalytic path to offering atypically gendered children even a rudimentary protection from being surveilled, overdiagnosed, and pathologized rooted a core sense of gendered self in a biological bedrock.

In the wider culture too this concept of a biologically ingrained gender identity became, and continues to be, a prominent rhetorical claim. To explain what we mean, let us flesh out the context in which the born-this-way argument arose and circulates. Born-this-way (the idea that gay people and atypically gendered people do not become but are born/have always been gay/trans, etc.) was originally meant to insulate LGBTQ people from the charge that their gender/sexual identity could be different if they worked hard enough, if they got the "right" treatment, if they socialized with the "right" people, if they had the "right" relationship to God, if they stayed out of gay bars or off the internet, and so on (Serano 2022). Versions of born-this-way arguments are offered to resist all these accusations as they arise in myriad social interactions.

Born-this-way has thus been an answer to some particular and threatening questions—namely, "can one catch homosexuality?" and "is trans contagious?" But the answer was not "invented" from scratch. Questions about why someone is gay/trans/insert-your-non-normative-identity-here are always answered by pulling on widely circulating ideas, stories, tropes, and myths in the social surround. This is what Laplanche called the "mythosymbolic" realm, the collective set of myths, symbols, and narrative structures "presented to the human being by his cultural surroundings" (2011, 247), by means of which the human being makes meaning. The mythosymbolic, in other words, is what all individuals, queer and not, draw on to arrive at their own self-theorizations, which is another way of saying that born-this-way is not necessarily a consciously deployed strategy but can nevertheless feel genuinely true to the subject. As such, the dominant cultural trope of inborn sexuality/gender strengthens the narrative that many queer subjects weave about the felt true-ness of their own gender/desires—and then recite to researchers, doctors, analysts.[7] This is

---

[7] That gender and sexuality are experienced and narrated through a vocabulary of "truth" and "true feeling" can be considered with reference to particular cultural and historical surroundings. Foucault (1978) directs our attention to how, in Western modernity, the will to know the truth of "sex" (one's own "sex" as well as the truth of the other's) is enfolded in relations of power. And gender clinics vividly demonstrate how truth claims about gender and sexuality are embedded in power relations. Doctors serve as gatekeepers, determining who will or will not receive access to transition-related medical care. In such a context, truth claims are also a game of strategy; trans subjects have to consider what version of truth (i.e., "true" identity) doctors need to hear, and may tactically contort their reports to fit existing medical models *in order to get the care they need*. For a vivid depiction of this dynamic, see *Framing Agnes* (2022), an experimental documentary that draws on previously

how myths around gender and sexuality get solidified, as each self-articulation feeds back into the reservoir of mythosymbolic cultural narratives that they were partly drawn from to begin with. A feedback loop is thus created by and through the mythosymbolic. Obviously, this loop is not unbreakable, otherwise we would never see any new gender forms, nor would any new translational codes ever emerge (Saketopoulou 2020a; Scarfone, forthcoming).

In the United States, born-this-way claims have been part of the rhetorical armature to ensure rights and protections for sexual and gender minorities. Without the cover of immutability, it is thought, sexual and gender diversities are prey to moral judgment and legal regulation (and therapeutic intervention). A body of work in legal studies and queer studies has contested the effectiveness—as well as the legal necessity—of asserting immutability to secure equal protections and freedom for historically despised groups (see, for example, Clarke 2015; Halley 1994; Jakobsen and Pellegrini 2004). Although born-this-way arguments have not fully succeeded in legal decisions or in the court of public opinion, this rhetoric has nevertheless accomplished something else: whatever stance one adopts in the born-this-way/warped-this-way divide,[8] thinking outside its binary terms has become a near

unseen archival research at UCLA.

[8] By *warped-this-way*, we refer to the widely held notion that atypical genders are a deviation from gender's normal course (i.e., a cis course wherein gender assignment and gender experience ostensibly

impossibility. It is in this context that the mere suggestion that psychic factors contribute to how one becomes trans, nonbinary, or genderqueer threatens to endanger the safety and rights of gender-diverse people. This is because such a suggestion is quickly construed to authorize attempts to eliminate atypically gendered experiences and identities.

This binary choice (acquired-and-therefore-possible-to-eliminate versus immutable-and-therefore-fixed) has also seeped into the culture of psychoanalytic theorizing. We can hear it humming beneath anxieties over "social contagion" and rapid-onset gender dysphoria (Bell 2020; Evans and Evans 2021) and in work that sees transness as a deviation from "normal gender" caused by trauma, as if atypical genders are those bent out of gender's proper shape (D'Angelo 2020). The only alternative to seeing diversity as a warping of normality has seemed to be a doubling down: true homosexuality and true transness are innate, and the existence of queer children proves it (Ehrensaft 2020, 2021).[9]

We want to offer a way around this impasse: it is possible to retrospectively discuss what factors *may* have played a role in someone becoming gender nonconforming

coincide). As we have been arguing, however, there is no "normal" course to gender nor is cis identity a "normal" or expectable gender course; again, *all* gender formations arise out of dynamic processes. (We offer additional criticisms of some of the conceptual and normative shortcomings of the term *cisness* in our next chapter.)

[9] Think, for example, of how early signs of transness are cited as evidence that one was "always" or "truly" trans.

TRAUMA AS RESOURCE

or sexually queer without this meaning that their difference is a problem to be "fixed." We believe that the field is in dire need of analytic ideas that don't capitulate to the notion that the only way to counter the pathologizing of sexual and gender non-normativities is by imagining them to be innate. *Nor is it humane to regard variant genders and sexualities without the resource of psychic complexity that psychoanalysis routinely affords to normative subjects.*

Thinking about gender as encompassing processes of becoming as opposed to ontological ones is clinically important and theoretically exciting. Being able to formulate clinical hypotheses about how someone's gender (normative or not) came into being can illuminate possible developmental paths that could, in turn, clinically support the flourishing of our atypically gendered patients. One of the reasons such patients (oftentimes rightly) do not trust our field is the rampant transphobia within psychoanalysis (see Hansbury 2017b; Pula 2015). But another important factor is that even clinicians who do not work toward eliminating atypical gender may become beset by so much anxiety in working with genderqueer patients that affirming the patient's gender and/or noting the trauma it has occasioned (through discrimination, violence, policing, etc.) are the furthest they'll go in their explorations. This attitude impoverishes what we, as a field, can offer our queer and trans patients.

On more than one occasion, we have found ourselves with patients who describe difficult, traumatic events in their lives, such as extreme parental intrusiveness or sexual violation. In the privacy of the consulting room, some such patients *need* to explore whether there may be links between these experiences and their genders. Any effort to do so is understandably fraught with tremendous shame and exorbitant anxiety, but when patients feel safe (i.e., that the analyst will not seize on the link to question the patient's gender), it becomes possible to explore memories, affects, and experiences that are otherwise unreachable.[10] The psychic work that can happen in this terrain, our clinical experience shows us, is deep and substantive: addressing otherwise recalcitrant feelings of shame around gender can soften the patient's own fears that their gender is damaged as a result of a psychic lesion,[11] as opposed to being just one possible response to such a lesion.

The ongoing homotransphobia of much psychoanalytic theorizing makes working this way both challenging and dangerous, because thinking trauma alongside gender diversity easily capsizes into conversion attempts. But, why? Why is it that analysts can work so skillfully with cis patients in ways that consider how trauma inflects

---

[10] We can't emphasize enough that such exploration needs to follow the patient's timeline *and initiative*, not the analyst's press or conviction.
[11] For some trans subjects, shame and worry that they have been destroyed by trauma may intensify self-hatred, making conversion attempts ego-syntonic. Ky Schever's experience (2020) is one such poignant example of how conversion therapies may appeal to individuals who are told that their transness or queerness was caused by untreated trauma and who are wooed by the promise of being "returned" to "normality."

cis femininities and cis masculinities,[12] but these same analysts cannot apply the same principles when working with gendered and sexual minorities without tipping into trying to eliminate difference? The answer seems obvious: cis genders are seen as natural and, where trauma does occur, such trauma is seen as part of the vicissitudes of (normative) gender. Atypical genders, on the other hand, are seen a priori as abnormal and, as such, any trauma is seen as warping "normal" gender to produce a distorted one. What we need to question, then, is the presumed naturalness of cis gender, and not to continue to impoverish conversations about gender and sexual polymorphism.

THE BACKDROP

IT IS IMPORTANT TO REMEMBER that we practice psychoanalysis and live in cultures that still harbor genocidal fantasies of a world with as few gay, lesbian, trans, and queer people as possible (Gill-Peterson 2018; Sedgwick 1990, 1991), and indeed with as few gay, lesbian, trans, and queer analysts and candidates as possible. For this reason, we are advocating for a psychoanalytic stance that marvels and *learns from* the persistence with which non-normative subjects appear before the analyst, determined to sustain being who they understand themselves to be despite considerable pressure and hostility from without.

---

[12] See this volume's preface for a detailed discussion.

Such is our attitude about the child whose clinical treatment we will soon discuss.

If, in the course of an analytic treatment, some sexual or gendered identification does shift, it is because the analytic work galvanizes new *self*-theorizations.[13] To be clear, however, even those shifts are not about the uncovering of some natural or essential truth about the subject. *All* gender formations are psychically meaningful *appearances* with material and psychic consequences. To say that gender is an appearance is not to say that gender is illusory or can be changed at will, but that gender is, rather, about how something psychic appears phenomenally. What makes gender experience real is that it exists on the level of psychic reality, where, experienced *as truth,* it becomes central to one's sense of self. Even as psychic reality, however, gender identification also requires the oxygen of relational recognition—including the analyst's (and the next chapter touches on that vis-à-vis the analyst's use of pronouns). We do well to remember that psychic reality is provisional, not a fixed state but a potentially mobile one; it is precisely that mobility, as we'll see in the clinical case, that implicates the subject's becoming and the subject's autonomy.

---

[13] We italicize *self* here to stress that we are speaking only about transformations that proceed *from processes that unfold in the subject and that embroil their unconscious life*, as opposed to issuing from the analyst's wishes or desires, however well-meaning or "therapeutic" the analyst understands them to be.

We use the phrase *psychic reality* as a psychoanalytic term that is irreducible to psychological or social reality. Psychic reality belongs to the order of translation, which means that it "is not created by me [the subject]; it is invasive" (Laplanche 1993/2015, 44). By *invasive,* Laplanche is referring to the intervention of the other's sexual unconscious, "compromising" conscious messages of gender assignment (as in: "It's a boy!" or "It's a girl!"). This introduces not a conflicted message (e.g., the mother had a boy but really wanted a girl, so she sent conflicted messages, and thus the child got "confused"—a warped-this-way account), but a *scrambled* one. This scrambling is always already sexual, and that is precisely what makes gender a site of innovation, because *all gender* is constructed out of the raw materials of what the other wants from (or for) us. Said differently, the other's invasion does not *determine* who we become. Rather, that invasion sets in motion the very process of our subjectivation; it is, rather, the response to this puncturing that consolidates as the ego, and also our experience of our gender.

As we'll see when we discuss Laplanche's model of gender, *all* subjects have to negotiate that puncturing. What distinguishes minoritarian subjects from those of dominant sexualities or genders is not the puncturing itself (that is, minoritarian subjects are not necessarily more traumatized or less able to handle the trauma). Rather, the self-theorizations minoritarian subjects invent in their effort to psychically negotiate that invasiveness are often turned against them.

PATIENT AFFIRMATION

"[U]NDER THE INSISTENCE THAT THE adult must protect the adolescent," Gozlan comments regarding the clinical literature on trans children, "two positions are presented: wild affirmations or wild condemnations" (2021, 174). Both, he continues, "represent the analyst's different anxieties with regards to how to think about the adolescent's agency, autonomy, and future" (ibid.). Against this wild affirmation/wild condemnation divide, we follow Gozlan's lead toward a third position, proposing the term *patient affirmation* to describe it. We here deliberately blur the adjectival and noun meanings of "patient" to speak of a kind of affirmation that, contrary to its wild variants, is neither simplistic nor rushed.[14] Patient affirmation follows rather than leads the patient, adopting the ethical stance of affirming *not the patient's identity, but the patient's right to have their own, nonlinear process*, which may or not be legible to the analyst or to other adults. (In our opinion, it is often the analyst's therapeutic response to this self-theorizing process that needs improvement.) Patient affirmation is thoughtful and makes use of the slowness of the process, without that amounting to a cautionary slowing down that is forced upon the patient, as in, for example, the "watchful waiting" approach that "gender

---

[14] We think of wild affirmation as traumatic response *and* manic defense, though we do not have time to explore this further here.

exploratory" models demand.[15] Nor does it presume a final destination for gender or sexuality.

If there is no final destination to gender, we may arrive at our gender not once and for all, but over and over again. For some individuals, gender could shift more than once

[15] We are referring here to the Gender Exploratory Therapy Association's (GETA) recently proposed model of working with gender, which advocates a "back-to-basics" approach vis-à-vis work with gender complexity, urging clinicians to use their "basic training about how to do therapy." GETA's exploratory therapy states that it is "open to a variety of outcomes, meaning we do not necessarily think that...identifying with one's birth gender is the desired outcome, nor do we think that celebrating a trans identity is the only necessary outcome, so working from this approach means that the client has all of his or her options open." GETA clinicians thus proclaim that their proposed framework is a reasonable and open-minded one. Their organizing premise is that "gender exploratory therapy...appreciates th[at] gender dysphoria can emerge in a context....So like all other kinds of distress there's a developmental, a family, a relational, a social context, and so in helping the client with that thorough process we want to give them lots of different lenses to understand the contextual way that their gender dysphoria emerged." As we'll soon explain, although we absolutely agree that there is a social context, a family background, a relational undercurrent in which gender unfolds—and that these at times include traumatic experience—we see these as being implicated in *all* gender formations. In singling out variant genders to be uniquely targeted by their approach, "gender exploratory therapy" reveals itself not to be the capacious and outcome-agnostic process it claims, but a stealthily constricted and constricting one. Their "advoca[cy] of...extended periods of time," so that comorbid conditions may be ruled out, positions the therapist as judge and decision maker of what is and is not about gender, placing the clinician's judgment at the decisional epicenter of how treatment and transition access should proceed. (These quotations are sourced from https://gender-a-wider-lens.captivate.fm/episode/96-official-launch-clinical-guide-for-therapists-working-with-gender-questioning-youth.)

across the lifespan. This makes trying to predict whether a patient may "regret" their transition an impossibility; as analysts, we have to accept that we do not have the special power of prophesizing the patient's future. For the same reason, we believe it more accurate to speak not of de-transitioning (as if the patient were returning to an "earlier" and "true" gender), but as *re*-transitioning. The latter term better gets at gender's evolutive potential (Hansbury and Saketopoulou 2022).

If we view gender as a matter of self-theorizing and not some true "core," it becomes possible to imagine that trauma can inflect gender experience *without* implying that this amounts to a distortion of an authentic self, as conversion therapies espouse (as in +Evans and Evans 2020). Put differently, we are pushing back against the assumption that gender is immune to trauma, or that gender, in order to be healthy, is uncontaminated by early traumatic intrusions, by adult interventions, or by the emotional debris of intergenerational pressures. As our theorization of the patient we call Ory will illustrate, the duress of the intergenerational transmission of trauma is not in and of itself sufficient to proclaim pathology: traumatic incursion is *always* at work in *all* gender-becoming. As long as the subject is able to modify what was handed down to them intergenerationally, and to forge out of those inheritances their own gender translations, gender is not pathology. To say this differently, no gender is unspoiled by trauma or uncontaminated by parental conflict. It is what the child *does* with those experiences (of trauma, intergenerational transport, etc.), how they are *spun into gender*, and whether such spinning acquires some autonomy from the original intrusion, that determines whether one's gender will feel viable, whether it will acquire the density of feeling like one's own.

Contemporary controversies over gender diversity both within and without psychoanalysis can force psychoanalytic theorists to retreat to clichés or to fearfully cling to simple, seemingly safer narratives. But what psychoanalysis needs—if it is going to remain relevant and if it is going to promote and uphold queer flourishing—is to venture into deeper thinking that can weather and contain the complexity of human life. "It is time," as Laplanche urges in the epigraph to this volume, "to abandon slogans and think on our own" (1992). We advocate for thinking about development dynamically, without falling into developmentalism. The latter implies "a succession of steps or stages," as if development were an unfolding of "potentialities already present [that] reveal themselves in a predetermined order" (Laplanche 1987, 66). Attending to development dynamically thus involves not tracking an expected, progressively maturational sequence, but rather paying close attention to how such sequences are undergirded by the sexual unconscious.

This querying of development, then, is not about noting where things "went off course" so that analysts may intervene to course-correct, nor does it mean identifying where psychic life got "bent out of shape" so that it may be straightened out. Instead, we seek to foster spaces for thinking about the evolving, dynamic dimensions of how patients—children especially, but also adults—change over time and come to their own idiosyncratic gender translations, especially those that may not line up with binary or gender-expansive dictionaries. Such thinking offers entry points for the analyst who has done the serious personal work of thinking about gender overall, *and their own in particular*, to engage their atypically gendered patients in more nuanced ways.

FIRST ENCOUNTERS

ILANA CAME TO SEE ME (A.S.) at the recommendation of Dr. P, a psychologist who was treating Ilana's older son, Henry. Dr. P had helped with Henry's history of severe anxiety, which had been fueling his serious school refusal, a problem previous treatments had failed to impact. As far as Ilana was concerned, Dr. P had restored Henry to "normality," a word that she used several times in our initial meeting to explain to me how, under my colleague's care, Henry was able to attend school again. This therapeutic success had resulted in her solid trust in Dr. P's opinion and methods, yielding a positive transference that had mounted to a near-hagiographic idealization. When their younger son, Ory, began to struggle and Dr. P confidently recommended me, Ilana was determined to follow his guidance to the letter. Before we even met, she developed an idealizing transference toward me that involved the expectation that I too would be equally effective in treating Ory.

Per Ilana's description, Ory, the youngest of eight siblings, suffered from being "too effeminate." His girlie presentation disturbed Ilana and her husband, both deeply religious people who found their child's demeanor to contradict "their family values." Ory brought unwelcome attention and the potential for shame to the family; his delicate mannerisms, feminine presentation, and high-pitched voice were seen by the parents as creating a "mountain of other problems, including severe anxiety and social difficulties." These "problems," Ilana explained, included a tendency to want to isolate, not playing sports with other boys, being "overly worried" about others' impressions of him, and an inclination to become preoccupied with matters that should not concern him—such as fashion. I privately wondered if this array of "symptoms" might relate to this young child's anxiety about his gender presentation, feelings of shame about his femininity, and fears of being unwanted.

Discussing the referral at length with me, Dr. P had shared his impression that Ory was likely a trans child who was being stifled by his parents and needed help coming out. Ory's parents' hope, as may already be clear, was different: that I could help course-correct their son so that he might behave as a "normal" boy who would eventually marry a "normal" girl, have "normal" children, and live a recognizable form of family life within the confines of their religious community.

Parental attitudes toward boyhood femininity have seen a tectonic shift in the past fifteen years. In New York City, where both of us practice, fewer and fewer parents are requesting help "straightening out" their children. Most seek help about how to best support their children, which oftentimes involves parents asking therapists to diagnose what relates to gender and what relates to early forms of sexuality that first become detectable as gender. Psychoanalysts get caught up in this too: the issue of whether a child is protogay or prototrans is one of the most frequent and complex clinical questions currently preoccupying psychoanalysts treating children with atypical gender presentations. However, the question "Is this child 'really' trans or 'really' gay?" treats gender and sexuality as stable ontological essences—as if, with the right protocols or diagnostic probes, one could conceivably discern another's "true" gender or sexuality. The gay versus trans distinction is problematically premised on the well-established analytic falsehood that sexuality and gender are separable from each other.

We believe that in the clinical setting, psychoanalysts need to let this question go. That said, parents' wish to know whether their child is gay or trans also has a pragmatic dimension: the hope is that an answer can inform their own stance and help them manage their child's environments (such as schools, social milieus, extended family, etc.) to prevent the negative mental health outcomes associated with gender variance, such as anxiety, depressive disorder, and the most frightening, suicidality (Spack et al. 2012; Turban and Ehrensaft 2018). This is understandable, and yet the wish to know whether a child is gay or trans often results in parents pressing for answers in ways that are premature for the child—and that analysts often feel they have to cave in to (a tendency we would urge against).

This anxious adult search for certainty means that in New York City, for example, it is becoming more common to meet parents who have trouble admitting to themselves—and thus to the analyst—the more conflicted feelings they may have about their child's gender non-normativity. The worry seems to be that their ambivalence will compromise care or support, or worse, that it will endanger their child's well-being. This set of reactions is culturally and geographically bound. In much of the United States, the United Kingdom, and many other parts of the world, the search for certainty oftentimes tilts in the opposite direction with parents seeking reassurance that their child is gay, not trans. Still, in the city where Ory and his family live, a seemingly unconflicted parental expectation for a child to be cleansed of their atypical gender presentation is more unusual.

The encounter with Ory's family was a meeting of two worlds that do not often intersect: the secular landscape of psychoanalysis, and a particular religious world in which gender and sexuality may have meanings illegible to many psychoanalytic practitioners. The lack of attention in our field to religiously inflected ideas about gender and sexuality can alienate religious families seeking help with gender nonconforming children, driving parents instead to community and religious leaders who are less experienced—and oftentimes untrained—in working with struggles around sexuality and gender. Not infrequently, treatments that boil down to conversion therapies are recommended, with the attendant traumatizing effects being well documented (Beckstead 2012; Meanley et al. 2020).

In the Orthodox Jewish community to which Ory's family belonged, there is still scant room for gender and sexual nonconformity. A conversation has been underway in the Orthodox world for the past few decades about LGBTQ issues, with the development of organizations, such as Eshel, dedicated to the needs of Orthodox LGBTQ individuals and their families. TransTorah—a self-described "collective of rabbis, teachers, educators, and cultural workers"—has created an online resource (transtorah.org) that "helps people of all genders to fully access and transform Jewish tradition, and helps Jewish communities to be welcoming sanctuaries for people of all genders" (http://transtorah.org/index.html). Such developments notwithstanding, Orthodox Judaism continues to struggle with how to make room for the lived experience of LGBTQ members (Slomowitz and

Feit 2019), making Eshel's vision for "a world where Orthodox LGBTQ individuals can live out their lives in the Orthodox communities of their choice" (https://www.eshelonline.org/eshels-mission/) a distant goal.

It is important to remember, however, that although Orthodox Judaism holds conservative ideas about gender and sexuality, religion is plural. Being religious does not necessarily amount to being conservative and restrictive when it comes to gender and sexuality (Alpert 2000; Frank, Moreton, and White 2018; Jakobsen and Pellegrini 2004; White 2015). In fact, there is great diversity across religions on LGBTQ issues—and *within* them too. Orthodox, Conservative, and Reform Judaisms are not all of the same mind on the halachic (Jewish legal) status of homosexuality and same-sex marriage, for example. Nor is Orthodox Judaism itself a monolithic entity; there are significant differences across the spectrum of ultra- and modern-Orthodox communities on these issues (Slomowitz and Feit 2019).

Even beneath what may seem like uniformity of ritual or belief to an outsider, there is in fact some room for variation—idiosyncratic innovation—in the layered ways that individuals (Ladin 2018) and families live out deeply held religious commitments. For example, the traumatic force of a particular religion's prohibitions on homosexuality or insistence on binary gender can be lightened or reconfigured in a family that is more flexible in its interpretation of sacred texts and that seeks advice from rabbis who are especially thoughtful on such issues. Membership in a conservative religious community, then, is not itself predictive of negative health outcomes for LGBTQ children or adults (Barringer and Gay 2017; Rosik et al. 2021). All this makes it especially important for clinicians working in secular contexts to be curious about the religious lives of their patients, in the same way we would be curious about the meanings of any other cultural context that inflects our patients' lives.

ILANA

WHEN I (A.S.) MET ILANA for an initial consultation, she impressed me as an incredibly thoughtful and caring mother who had seemingly selflessly devoted herself to the care of her eight children. In our initial consultation, Ilana recounted a dizzying schedule of driving one kid after another from school, to private lessons, to violin practice, to basketball games, and to multiple therapy appointments. It was clear that she was overwhelmed, as well as determined to manage it all stoically and without complaint: Ilana was committed to the role of the quietly suffering mother. Her marriage appeared to be structured along very traditional gender roles, with her husband, Aaron, leaving early for work and returning late at night with little participation in the everyday care of the children. Ilana welcomed his numerous corrective comments regarding her handling of Ory, whose girlishness, Aaron felt, Ilana did not sufficiently reprimand. Ilana nervously confessed to me that she feared that her son's femininity was her fault, and wondered if she had encouraged it by not more firmly disciplining him for his "effeminate" speech or gestures.

I soon learned that while most of her eight children had struggled at some point with anxiety, her oldest son, Henry, had been the most symptomatic. By age fourteen, Henry's anxiety had overwhelmed most aspects of his functioning, and he refused to attend school. When numerous therapeutic interventions failed, the parents decided to send him to boarding school. This, Aaron felt, would ensure school attendance and also "teach" him the lesson he needed: that his acting out would not be tolerated. Ilana had been ambivalent about this decision, agreeing reluctantly and at her husband's insistence— though, as we will see, that ambivalence was more layered than she was aware. Henry deteriorated gravely while in boarding school. It was only in retrospect and with Dr. P's help that the parents came to understand that sending him to boarding school had been experienced by Henry as a violent expulsion, an eviction from his home and his family. Much of Henry's treatment, Ilana explained, revolved around processing that trauma and trying to undo the effects of that parental message.

Although I learned much in these first meetings about Ory's family's dynamics that would ultimately prove useful, it was also clear that Ilana was hesitant to bring Ory in to see me. On the manifest level, this was related to the family's recent experience of having consulted with a colleague who, never having met Ory, told them that he was likely trans. The parents felt that this diagnosis was rushed and based on insufficient information. It was also clear to me that such a possibility would have been very unwelcome in this family. The parents wanted the right therapist who could help "prevent" both homosexuality and transness, and this, I came to realize, was what I was being vetted for.

During our meetings, Ilana described Ory as a sensitive boy with multiple learning and emotional issues. It was clear from the way she spoke about him that she loved him dearly and felt especially protective of him. Ory seemed to have a special place in her heart. This, experience has taught me, is often the case for children who are unconsciously slotted by the parent to perform an important psychic function for them (an issue we will return to shortly). At the same time, it was also clear that Ilana was frustrated with this child whose femininity in speech, gesture, and habits she found uncomfortable and confusing. Plus, Ilana worried that she would be forever blamed for his gender complexity. In fact, Aaron and her parents attributed it to her difficulty setting boundaries with him. Ory's femininity, Ilana explained, was now becoming disruptive to the family's unity. Aaron, often impatient with him, had become abrupt and sharp in his manner of addressing Ory. As a result, Ilana reported, Ory was increasingly irritated and avoidant of his father, clinging to her in ways that further fueled Aaron's concern that the mother-son tie was overly close. Ory's siblings were more and more embarrassed to be seen in public with him and had begun avoiding him in school. One sister worried that Ory's presentation would compromise her marriage prospects, and the parents shared this fear, which, they told me, was entirely realistic in their community. Ilana impressed upon me how important the family's reputation was to her and her husband, putting public appearances with the children under a magnifying glass. Ory's gender behaviors imperiled the standing of the extended family as well. The public dimension of Ory's gender nonconformity was thus endowed with profound religious meanings.

Ilana recognized that expecting a 12-year-old to carry the family reputation on his slim shoulders was a lot. Over the course of my many contacts with her I came to respect her struggle. And struggle she did: despite wanting to do right by her child, she also frequently found herself helplessly exasperated with him. "I don't understand why he does those things," she would say, enumerating a long list of "girly" behaviors: a subtle but persistent flick of the wrist, an especially high-pitched voice that she was sure was "put on," a certain gracefulness in his gestures when he would straighten out his clothes, a particular kind of laughter that seemed, she whispered to me, "kind of gay." She told me that she had instructed him to sit on his hands since he couldn't help himself from gesturing, and that she had asked him, even begged him, not to speak in "this high-pitched voice that drives his father crazy." Ilana could see that these interventions were ineffective and upsetting to Ory and left him feeling criticized and surveilled. She felt frustrated with herself for making them, but was also confused because she believed that Ory was acting that way intentionally—to annoy her, to create parental conflict, and to draw attention to himself. At other times, I would get heartfelt, self-aware emails from her about how clear it was to her (at those moments) that the struggle was hers, not a fault in Ory but a difficulty in herself. In these notes, she lamented subjecting her child to her behavior, which she also felt she could not help. Unlike parents who use the "this is too hard for *me*" line as alibi to do no work on themselves, Ilana's words felt genuine to me.

Unsurprisingly, Ory had recently started refusing to have any conversations with her about his "behaviors," which further distressed her. As a result, she was also doubtful that he would talk to me. I, too, felt that his femininity had become so much a focus that talking about his feelings about it or his family's reactions might feel as if he were being monitored by yet another adult. More than anything, I felt pessimistic that there would be enough time to allow a therapeutic process to unfold; these parents wanted Ory's gender "cleaned up," seeking the kinds of magical results that my colleague had produced with Henry's symptoms, and that I could neither guarantee nor endorse.

In my joint meeting with both parents, I suggested

to them that Henry's having been sent away to boarding school likely had an impact on Ory as well. Might it have fueled fears that he too could be expelled from the family home if his behavior did not align with parental expectations? I further noted that their obvious displeasure at his gender presentation might make him feel precarious. While I was explaining that any therapeutic endeavor would have to prioritize his emotional well-being rather than being invested in any one particular gender outcome, Aaron briskly interrupted me: "You should know that if he becomes a homosexual, he would *not* be welcome in our home. It's not like we would have him over for family dinner with his boyfriend; that's not the kind of family we have. It's not the life we live. And I don't mean he'd have to leave when he grows up," he added with force, "but as soon as it's clear that that's where he is heading."

This manifesto stunned me. I quickly took inventory of what I knew about this family. I couldn't imagine that Ilana would altogether refuse her son, but I could also see that standing up to Aaron would be no easy task. The meeting left me heartbroken and scared for Ory. How could I, in good conscience, do the work that this child would need, when that work could conceivably lead in a direction that spelled a family catastrophe or an abandonment? I could discern no opening in this family that might, over time and with work, become a path to accepting their child, were Ory to come to identify as gay, genderqueer, or trans. Both Dr. P and I had by now recommended that Ilana enter individual treatment (she had refused), and neither of us could imagine suggesting this to the father without risking serious rupture.

MEETING ORY

I MET WITH ORY'S PARENTS for almost three months before they decided it was time for him to come and meet with me.

Unusually pretty and vulnerable-looking, Ory carried himself in an intensely shy and reserved manner that seemed self-protective. Under the external presentation of polite deference, I could discern his reflexive tendency to organize himself around what he sensed others expected of him. As early as the first meeting, his inclination to want to please manifested in our relationship, as well as his fear that human bonds were too fragile to sustain difference, or worse, tension. He was reluctant to take initiative or indicate any interests that might shape our session; he did not look through my board games or books as some children his age tend to do. He replied courteously to my gentle inquiries by quickly turning them into queries about *my* likes and *my* preferences, all the while sitting obediently on the couch with his hands crossed across his lap (perhaps to keep them from betraying his girlishness?) while waiting to be instructed what to do.

Suffice it to say that the initial period was strained. Ory, I felt, was coming because his parents expected him to. In the transference, I had become the parent to whom he would demonstrate his compliance. Several awkward sessions into a treatment that was proceeding with many uncomfortable silences, Ory one day relaxed his hands, letting them fall to the side, touching my couch. In the stillness that regularly filled the room, I noticed him running his fingers over the fabric. I commented on its softness and asked him how the fabric felt on his skin. To my surprise, Ory proceeded to describe in intricate detail the sensation on his fingers. I was impressed with the sensuality in his use of language. After a rather long exchange about the fabric of the couch, I commented with admiration that he seemed to know so much about how things felt on his skin. In retrospect, my comment may seem too intimate, too embodied for such a reluctant and cautious child, but in the tenor of the conversation at the time, it made intuitive sense. Ory responded with a shy, content smile. Something in him opened up.

Speaking spontaneously for the first time, Ory started telling me about a small collection of fabric pieces that he kept hidden in a bag in his bedroom. I asked about them. He became animated in describing their textures, and soon he started leading me around the room, instructing me to touch objects, fabrics, and plants that might convey to me the feel of the particular softness of one, the velvety texture of another, the way another swished when the wind blew on it softly. We talked about his fabrics for several sessions. I learned where he found them, how he picked them, which ones he preferred and why. One day, as he was struggling to find the right word to describe the precise color of his latest acquisition, I asked whether he might want to bring his prized bag to our session and show me his fabrics. Ory quickly retreated. His face darkened. His parents, he told me, did not know about this bag. They would not like him having it, and they could not find out about it. Plus, Ory explained, he could not imagine how he could sneak it in. I was pleased that sneaking it in, even if not something he could do, was something he could imagine; it suggested to me a capacity to separate, at least in his mind, from his parents' wishes for him. Ory volunteered that he did not know why his parents would be dismayed at this collection. I wondered to myself if he knew more about their displeasure than he was ready to discuss openly with me, or to acknowledge to himself.

In a session soon thereafter, Ory was guiding me through the room when he reached into my toy chest—this too was a first. He retrieved a doll, and, rubbing the fuzzy fabric of her dress, he likened it to how orchid petals felt. But, he added hurriedly, you are not supposed to touch them because of how sensitive they are: "touching the petals can kill the plant." I was intrigued by this uncharacteristic outpouring that, in the following sessions, turned into an elaborate detailing of his love of orchids. That's how I learned that Ory's favorite preoccupation was researching orchids online and learning about their care, about different types and the delicate attention they require to survive, about their exquisite sensitivity to light and water, all of which, he told me, was reflected in the color of their roots, "if you know how to look." I admired his knowledge and asked him if he would be willing to teach me about them. "How?" he asked, bewildered. I suggested I get an orchid for my office that we could care for together. He took me up on it immediately. We went online, browsed through online orchid sellers, and decided together on the size and color of the plant. When Ory left the session, he said goodbye to me for the first time.

At our next meeting, Ory eagerly entered my office scanning the room to find the plant. He quickly located the white- and purple-speckled flowers. The plant had two stems, one of which was attached to a supporting plastic rod, while the other was less supported and slightly bent to the side. He was delighted and pronounced the plant "fabulous." With uncharacteristic pleasure, he proceeded to inspect its roots and advised me about placement and watering. It was, he told me, a healthy and strong plant. It would do very well in my office, he announced, a comment that I also heard as transferential. I asked him if there was anything we should be doing about the unsupported, bent stem. At the time, I didn't intend this statement as an intervention; in the moment, it felt like a genuine question addressed by me, the orchid novice, to him, the orchid expert. But when Ory instantly fell silent, I realized that what I'd said was more fraught.

After a few moments of silence, he volunteered that

his mother had also bought him an orchid. This was the first time he was referencing anything about his family life. That plant, he explained, had a single stem, and it was bent over, just like the one I had asked him about. "She tried to fix it," he said, "She broke it. It died." The tone in the room shifted. I waited. Then, he softly added, "I thought it had looked rather beautiful bent over." "Your mom seems to have felt it needed fixing," I said, gently, "but it sounds like it may have been beautiful just as it was. Bent." Ory looked at me, making eye contact for the first time. The session came to an end.

Ory never returned to see me.

AFTER ORY

ORY REFUSED TO COME TO his next two sessions, telling his mother that he wasn't finding our work helpful. I hypothesized that our exchange about the orchid and my comment about his mother might have approximated too much, putting in language too soon the sorts of fears that kept Ory quiet and compliant in our earlier sessions. A kind of psychic death, it seemed, awaited efforts to "fix" any deviation from straight, upright development. Had speaking to me about it made it too real for him? Or did the idea that space could exist in our work for these experiences to be articulated feel, perhaps, like too much of a threat to the relationship with his mother? Or, if I knew that plants could die that way, did that cement the truth of his suspicion? Or, or, or...the number of possible interpretations I have considered over time keep multiplying…

Unsurprisingly, Ory's father welcomed his decision to stop treatment. Not only had he begun feeling that his son should be seeing a male therapist if the point was, after all, to eradicate his femininity, but he was also becoming worried that, like Ory's mother, I was not good at setting appropriate limits on Ory's girlie-ness. Ilana similarly took too quickly to the idea that Ory needn't come back, not even for a goodbye session. She asked instead if I would see her regularly for "parenting advice." Hoping that this would keep a door open for Ory to return at some future point, I agreed.

As our individual "parenting" meetings began to accumulate, I heard less about Ory and more about Ilana's own early family history. Ilana spoke with admiration and pride about her religious heritage, which had afforded the family great respectability and which contributed to their social standing and professional success. Ilana also spent several sessions describing to me her relationship to God and to her faith. She was certain, she confided in me, that her deep belief in God and her prayers had been instrumental in healing her parents from the serious, life-threatening illnesses they had both suffered when she was a child.

It was only after Ilana was convinced I understood her deep commitments to her religion that she was able to tell me about the only period in her life when she had questioned her faith: a small "blip," she called it, in an otherwise incontestable record of religious devotion. Ilana described with uncharacteristically emotional language the distress and instability that questioning her religion and the existence of God had brought to her life. Lasting several months, this period found her noticing inconsistencies in sacred texts, and seeing glaring divergences between the teachings of religious figures and their ways of life.

The shock waves these doubts generated rippled through her entire being as she found herself panicked and ashamed to be having the thoughts at all. She began to question whether her relationships to her parents and siblings could survive if they knew of her preoccupation, and she agonized over what would happen if they became aware of her doubts. Would she be sent away for intensive religious instruction?[16] Sent to distant relatives to prevent her disobedience from becoming known? Might she even be turned out and shunned by her family? Ilana was frightened that she would bring shame and disrepute upon her family and dared speak to no one about this. Her anxiety mounted, giving way to episodes during which she felt as though she were endlessly falling. She described full-

---

[16] Ilana's fantasy about being sent away for instruction is not without realistic basis. In some contemporary Orthodox communities, doubt is seen as a psychological disturbance. Potential heretics may then be referred for therapeutic intervention with therapists who see such questioning as a sign of mental illness (Fader 2020; Seidman 2021).

blown panic attacks that kept her confined at home, unable to attend school. As she described her social isolation and the sense of helpless dysfunction that overtook her family, I noted the overlap with the symptoms that both Ory and her older son, Henry, had struggled with.

Ilana's crisis, I learned, occurred at age twelve, the same age as Ory when he was brought to see me. Her crisis mirrored the fears around shame and sudden separation that I suspected Ory was also experiencing—and that had also played out in the transference, I now saw. I wondered if her need to repair Ory's gender to an unimpeachable masculinity with no threat of queerness on the horizon— whether of sexuality or gender—functioned as a kind of symbolic reparation unconsciously extended to her father for her own lapses in "normality" when it came to conforming fully to the family's religious beliefs. What if Ilana's investment in her child's otherness, and in the process of cleansing him of it, were in part a displacement of her highly charged guilt around questioning the religion that her father, family, and culture so deeply believed in? Might Ory's gender hold for her both the "damage" she had done to her father in her fantasy by her "heretical" difference and the fantasized reparative gesture to him? If so, Ilana might have a conflictual investment in Ory's gender "dis-obedience": on the one hand, his femininity sustained the disobedience that she had to give up to be a dutiful daughter and not lose her family; on the other, by seeking to eliminate his femininity, she was "repairing" the damage risked by her own "phase" of noncompliance. Ilana was split: both invested in and adversarial to Ory's gender complexity.

Fantasies of reparation, such as Ilana's, may be one dynamic at play in some families, helping us understand the parent's deep and intractable investment in a child's normativity. They may help explain why parents who are otherwise loving and caring may appear self-righteous in their commitments to "cleanse" their children of their gender atypicality, even as this investment clearly overrides a child's emotional well-being. Put differently, Ilana's worries over Ory's gender not only reflected the commandments of her religious world, but bespoke her powerful and unconscious internal dynamics that were not originally about gender per se—at least not in any straightforward way. To be sure, gender is never straightforward; it is never, that is, "only" about gender.[17] In this case, gender is also about race and religion. More specifically, in questioning her religion, had young Ilana also felt herself to be challenging male authority to interpret religious ideas? If so, maybe Ilana too had once experienced her own version of gender trouble as refracted through religion—not in the sense of questioning her gender assignment, but in the sense of questioning received wisdom that she was prohibited by her gender from interrogating.

[17] This point has long been emphasized in critiques voiced by women of color feminists and trans of color critique (e.g., Bey 2020b; Crenshaw 1989; Snorton, 2017; Spillers 1987).

The overlay of religion, gender, and race in the modern history of anti-Semitism may make gender into an especially apt conduit for the kind of reparative fantasies discussed here. Numerous scholars have traced how modern anti-Semitism has imagined Jewish "difference" through the prisms of gender and sexuality, in effect "racing" gender/sex and "sexing" race/religion (Boyarin 1997; Geller 2007; Gilman 1991, 1993; Pellegrini 1997). The racial "sciences" of the late nineteenth and early twentieth centuries scrutinized the Jewish male body for proof of dangerous Jewish difference. In the anti-Semitic imaginary, a cluster of bodily signs—such as the "weak" Jewish foot with its "faulty" gait or the "corrupt" accent of the Jewish voice (Gilman 1991)—was held to expose the specific and negative distinction of "the Jew."

But the central "proof" of racialized Jewish difference was circumcision, which embodied the supposedly perverse sexuality and dubious, effeminate gender of Jewish men.[18] Many of the anti-Semitic stereotypes circling around Jewish (male) difference also became part of the medico-cultural repertoire for identifying sexual inversion and, later, homosexuality (Boyarin, Itzkovitz, and Pellegrini 2003).[19] Although most of this anti-Semitic

[18] In a footnote to the case of Little Hans, Freud himself argues for the crucial role that circumcision plays in anti-Semitic fantasies of Jewish difference (1909, 36n1). For a compelling reading of this footnote, see Boyarin (1997, 231-54).

[19] That Ory's parents were both particularly vexed by his distinctive "high-pitched voice," seeing it as a queer symptom of gender gone

discourse focused on Jewish men, the accusation that Jews did their gender "wrong" and their sexuality "perversely" has also negatively impacted Jewish women. These anti-Semitic and homophobic stereotypes have a violent, even genocidal, history. Could they have been part of the intergenerational transmission between Ilana and her son, in this instance as the transmission of a religio-racial trauma?

THE SEARCH FOR IDENTITY CATEGORIES

A SEA CHANGE OF CULTURAL shifts around gender and sexual non-normativity in adolescents, some of which have been enabled by advances in queer theory and trans studies, make it more common nowadays for adolescents to articulate solidified identity claims about being gay or trans. In instances when children are too young to make such claims, parents are already thinking about them—and perhaps downloading them into their children, foreclosing some possibilities even as they try to help craft others. It has become customary, as discussed earlier, for parents to be preoccupied with trying to ascertain whether a male-assigned child's feminine presentation, or a female-assigned child's masculinity, should be understood as early homosexuality or transness—and psychoanalysts also become entrenched in trying to diagnose this correctly.

---

wrong, may be an example of this crossover of anti-Semitic and homophobic stereotypes.

We believe such identity claims, when they are sought by the parent and especially when they are made by an adolescent or a child patient, have to be treated clinically with an appreciation of their nuanced complexity. We think it crucial that we don't read them flatly as straightforward, self-evident communications about a child's "true" nature.[20] By this, we do not mean to imply that such claims should be questioned as to their validity and treated by the analyst with suspicion or even antagonism, or that analysts are more competent arbiters of their patients' genders or sexualities. Rather, it is our view that psychoanalysis's increased willingness as a field to grant atypical presentations the legitimacy they deserve, and to bestow upon them what Salamon (2014) has poignantly called *the dignity of belief,* should not substitute for our enduring investment in understanding them as arising out of dynamic, object-related, psychic processes. We can, and should, do both: granting atypical genders and sexualities the dignity of belief is the *opening* condition for the analytic task of understanding what gender and sexuality mean for the patient and tending to the psychic work gender and sexuality do.

We are thus moving away from the typical focus in the analytic literature on gender as an accrual of identificatory or counteridentificatory processes, or as something

---

[20] Again, we do not subscribe to the notion of a "true" gender that, if one peels back the layers of defense or encrusted false-self formations, may be discovered at the self's core.

constituted through Oedipal crises, theories that have been both useful and well critiqued (Corbett 2007; Corbett, Dimen, Goldner, and Harris 2014; Gherovici 2019; González 2019; Gozlan 2008, 2015; Hansbury 2017; Harris 2008; Pula 2005; Suchet 2011). Rather, we hone our focus on factors that can be handed down intergenerationally, as may be the case with Ory and Ilana, and that can then be psychically bound *through* gender.[21] By attending to these kinds of nuances, psychoanalysts may be able to begin undoing the knots that tie our patients' genders to the other—for example, upholding parental coherence or protecting the parent from having to process her own trauma (Silverman 2016)—so that the patient's gender can feel more integrated, more like their own creation. In so doing, we may be able to help our patients be more in their gender, with less shame and more pleasure, inhabiting gender as an idiom of their own forging, even if their gender may have originated through the other, *as gender always does*.

To explain these points, we will need a short and careful journey through Laplanche, for whom gender is related to the ego's attempt to cope with the plenitudes of

---

[21] In saying that identification/counteridentification is not part of our thinking, we are not denying the role of object relations, but emphasizing that gendered features (e.g. a parent's femininity or another's exuberant affect) become more or less appealing as translational funnels *because* of the object ties through which the child was exposed to them and the relational context in which they were experienced.

the infantile sexual.[22] Gender, that is, works to bind and thus to render intelligible the excess of the infantile sexual, formatting the anarchic elements of the sexual drive through, among other things, gender codes that try to make the infantile into something that can be assimilated by the subject. In that sense, identity is a set of claims that announces something that is true enough for the subject. Let us briefly flesh out Laplanche's position in regard to gender, which we will then link to the clinical material.

For Laplanche (1987; reprinted in this volume) the attachment relationship between infant and caregiver operates on two simultaneous levels. The infant is the regular recipient of acts of parental care (feeding, diapering, etc.) that meet survival and instinctual needs and convey messages of care. These messages, however, are always parasitized by the parent's own sexual unconscious. The infant is invariably exposed to—and always unprepared for (Scarfone 2015)—the parent's sexual unconscious, which unremittingly compromises any and all communications to the infant, producing an enigmatic disturbance for the infant, a perturbation that Laplanche described as "a thorn in the flesh of the ego" (1970, 129). He thus described enigma as an irritant that's implanted in the infant's psychophysiological skin, a sting of sorts that generates an urgency for the infant to make meaning out of what

---

[22] We here direct the reader to Laplanche's important essay "Gender, Sex and the *Sexual*," which is reprinted as this volume's third chapter. Further references to this essay will appear in the main text.

has radiated out of the parent and into them. The child is impelled to make sense of this irritant and does so by "translating" the enigmatic surcharge. Because there is no "content" to enigma that can be accurately transcribed (enigma is unknowable to the parent as well), translation does not refer to some (accurate or inaccurate) decoding, but rather to the infant generating a fantasy (Scarfone 2016) that offers a good enough binding (*good enough* in the sense of sufficiently binding the enigmatic disturbance and being a good enough fit with the child's being). Enigma, however, cannot be fully culled by translation; some remainder always escapes. These remainders become repressed, constituting the sexual unconscious.

For Laplanche, the ego gets formed through the attempt to cope with the strangeness of the other by translating enigma. How do we translate enigma, however, if not by some reference to veridical translation, to the "thereness" of the parent's communications? The answer to this question is one of the most fascinating parts of Laplanchean theory: for its translational efforts, the infant borrows codes from the mythosymbolic, the cultural forms transmitted to the infant through the adults (Laplanche 2011; see also Aulagnier 1987). The child employs these codes to make sense of the adult world, and it is these translations that give rise to what we think of as unconscious fantasy (Scarfone 2016). These translations also sediment as ego, and, we would add, when the codes pertain to gender, as gender identity. Importantly, these codes are not of the child's own making; they are already nominated as possible translational funnels by existing cultural products, that is, through what is already socially and culturally intelligible.

Still, translations are also the child's own creations in the sense that it is the child's particular use and mixing of these codes that make their translations not a mere reproduction or regurgitation of the social world, but a rendering of the psychic world in their own personal idiom.[23] Infantile sexuality also becomes represented and, from there on out, yields identitarian experience by becoming structured in the grammar of culture (Evzonas 2020; Saketopoulou 2017b). Laplanche specifically understood gender as one such cultural object that is effortlessly—and, we would stress, with the appearance of naturalness—made available by the parents to the child, who then relies upon it to format their own translations (see Laplanche's chapter in this volume).

Laplanche uses the term *assignment* to gender to emphasize the primacy of the other in this process; this is the case, he says, "whether the first assignment is the declaration at the town hall, at the church, or in some other official place, a declaration involving the assignment of a first name, the assignment to a place in a kinship network, etc., or very often the assignment to membership

---

[23] It goes without saying that this is not a conscious, intentional process.

in a religion" (this volume 118). Though he speaks of "first assignment," he also stresses that assignment is "ongoing," not occurring in a singular moment, but rather through an ongoing "bombardment of messages" (119). Laplanche's mention of assignment to religious membership hints at ways gendered being may have a religious dimension, and vice versa.[24] The Jewish ritual of circumcision, or *brit milah*, is a powerful example of the twinned assignment to religion and gender. In fact, the *brit milah* commonly includes two important rituals: the circumcision itself, which marks the entry of the male Jewish child into the covenant, and a naming ceremony in which the boy's Hebrew name is announced, often for the first time. Religion and gender meet and co-articulate at the braid of word, body, and communal witnessing.

To underscore: although the ego necessarily makes use of materials available in the cultural surround to cope with the strain of enigma, this does not mean that we merely "download" from the mythosymbolic, reproducing it word for word. The codes furnished by caretakers are not "pure" but always already alloyed by the adults' own fantasy. Further, individuals can and frequently do stretch cultural forms, which facilitates their own idiosyncratic

[24] This is a tantalizing possibility that Laplanche raises again in footnote 6 in Appendix II of "Gender, Sex and the *Sexual*" (this volume). There he notes that "in certain countries the registration of a birth may involve other categories than that of gender," such as "racial assignment ('white'), religious assignment (Catholic, Muslim, no religion, etc.), racial-religious assignment, etc."

becomings. We see a powerful example of this in the work of poet and literary scholar Joy Ladin, a long-time English professor at Yeshiva University in New York City. At the time of her transition in 2008, Ladin was the first openly transgender employee of an Orthodox Jewish institution anywhere in the world. Ladin describes how Jewish notions of God's unrepresentability helped her younger self make sense of "being utterly, unspeakably different" (2018, 3). Ladin early on felt herself at painful odds with the boy her parents and others saw her to be. But, she writes, "God never mistook me for the body others saw… God, like me, had no body to make God visible, no face human beings could see" (2018, 2). We see in Ladin an unexpected—and to some, counterintuitive—psychic use of the Torah for the ego's translational activity, where "being transgender… brought me closer to God" (2018, 3).

Many concepts that we use to order the world—such as sexual orientation, race, ethnicity, class, and religion— can be thought of as "found objects" (Saketopoulou 2017b) taken up in the labor of translating the sexual unconscious. They offer us "processes of closure" against "destabilizing intimations of an awareness of the centrality of the other['s] unconscious" (Browning 2016, 1042) in our own being. But the closure these categories present is always incomplete (because the infantile sexual is never fully translated), which helps explain why so many of these concepts (such as race and gender) can feel hard to pin down, resisting language and crumbling when examined closely, betraying their unstable foundations. Still, such closure can give the sexual drive a linguistic coating and create the appearance of stable psychic structure. But it is important to remember that these translational codes and the Ptolemaic closure they offer always precede the subject's formation, and are thus never of one's own invention.

RETURNING TO ORY

IN THIS CONTEXT, WHAT IF we considered the possibility that Ory's gender is partly constructed through the particular way it is put to use in his mother's psyche? Might Ilana's need for Ory's non-normative gender as a placeholder for her own otherness—an otherness that would have been unacceptable to her family of origin and larger religious community, and that had to be actively suppressed—have become a translational code for Ory? Notably, both Henry and Ory end up with symptoms that speak not just to their own difficulties, but to Ilana's trouble: Henry, for instance, struggled with school attendance at the same age his mother underwent her period of religious doubt, and Ory similarly found himself in a place of anxiety about being ejected from his home and family. Could we think of Ory's gender as carrying the mother's own disavowed early conflicts regarding her relationship with her religion, complete with the fears of parental rejection and social isolation? Here, worry over the son's gender may be an especially powerful carrier of the mother's religious doubt, because gender "queerness" has been linked to Jewish difference in the larger cultural imagination.

Seriously examining these questions requires us to maintain a paradoxical tension. On the one hand, we would have to hold Ory's gender as an artifact of intergenerational transport, kept in place by the function it serves not in the self but in the object (in this case, Ilana). Ory's gender is in that sense an intergenerational errand, to use Apprey's term (2014). On the other hand, we have to keep that formulation in mind without turning Ory's gender into Ilana's symptom, that is, without rendering it into something alien to Ory by treating it as an imposition of parental fantasy that distorts Ory's "original" and "true" male gender. The latter would be reminiscent of those problematic strands of analytic theorizing that attribute gender complexity, which is read as gender failure, to parental conflict or trauma (e.g., Chiland 2000; Coates 1990; Socarides 1984).

We need to remember, instead, that *all* gender identities, including normative ones, are synthesized through codes that are not internal to the subject, but which become available through the other (the parent). Ory—no more than any other atypically *or* normatively gendered individual—is thus not alone in having a gender baked into him, which is inflected by the other's fantasies, wishes, or needs. This, we are arguing, is the starting condition of all genders, normative and non. In other words, we propose that what is transmitted intergenerationally is not content that passes nonverbally and stealthily across generations from one unconscious to the other. Memories and traumatic inscriptions in the older generation become part of the repertoire of codes the adult inadvertently makes available to the next generation, which are then taken up by the child in translating enigma.

It is important to underscore here the critical theoretical contribution this formulation makes to Laplanchean thinking overall. Oftentimes, the notion of enigma is misunderstood by readers of Laplanche as giving us the mechanism of how intergenerational transmission happens, aka through something "enigmatic." But this distorts Laplanche's idea, which is that enigma is by definition contentless. What, the question remains, is the relationship between enigma and intergenerational transmission? What impact, in the Laplanchean model, does intergenerational transport have on psychic formation? This is where we intervene, to argue that, yes, material is carried through the generations (e.g. Holocaust trauma, or the violences of slavery) but that is not a process on the level of enigma. To the contrary, such trauma is highly represented even if non-verbal or secondarily repressed. This highly represented material is related to the child through narrated stories about the past, or communicated nonverbally through the caretakers' affects, gestures, and disposition, and thus get added to the cultural and personal trove of codes that the child may then draw on to translate enigma. This is how the older generation's history becomes structuralized into a later generation's psychic life: through translational codes and not through enigma.

Psychoanalysis has historically looked at processes of intergenerational inheritances or transmissions as pathognomonic: we have treated them, that is, as indexing a parental wish that is *tasked to* the child and carried *as distortion* of the child's true self (Coates 1990; Coates and Moore 1988). In these kinds of theorizing, Winnicottian concepts of *true versus false self, and of genuine versus inauthentic experience,* explain how children can become the ventriloquists of parents' unresolved conflicts and familial ambivalences. This kind of thinking, when applied to gender, treats gender as a fixed entity, adhering to the notion of core gender identity critiqued earlier in this chapter. Such true, preexisting gender identity, the argument goes, is violated by the parent's unconscious deployment of their child. But as we have argued, a notion of a "true" gendered interiority that assumes gender to be a cryptogram waiting to be decoded by the right, competent reader is both unfounded and problematic. If gender is not its own primary, ontological category, but rather a set of translational codes through which the infantile sexual is bound, then we may profitably see gender as an emergent process that allows many twists and turns.

Gender translations, then, are not either right or not (matching the body's biological sex markers, the individual's gender assignment at birth, or their "true" sense of gender), but more a matter of a goodness of fit, a *degree* of match. As a culturally transmitted object that is elaborated through the parent's unconscious, *all* gender is definitionally inflected with parental emotional debris, and *all* gender positions in their efflorescence as well as their humiliations carry the batons of intergenerational conflicts. To think otherwise is to permit normative strivings to exert considerable regulatory pressures (Corbett 2011) on our metapsychology by imagining that some genders are unconstrained by personal history or cultural infiltrations.

To say this differently: whatever his mother needs Ory to be or not be—a boy (so that he and she may both be "normal"), or a non-normative or trans child (so her own otherness has somewhere to go)—Ory still has to craft a life despite his mother's fantasies/needs/how she uses him psychically.[25] The question of whether Ory is able or not to invent something out of Ilana's dynamics is, ultimately, the decisive factor as to whether he can become his own person. Critically, what we are dealing with is not a case of "Ory's mother has caused too much damage already, so the analyst needs to help Ory be okay with his 'bentness.'" Although we have no problem whatsoever with the notion that "one has to do something with the damage that's already been done,"[26] we maintain in this case *that there*

---

[25] We speak only of the mother here because not enough clinical data exists around Aaron, who, we assume, is also significantly contributing to these dynamics.

[26] For in-depth discussions of this idea, see Saketopoulou's notion of *traumatophilia* (2023a, 2023b).

is no "damage" done. Parents (in this case Ory's mother, but really, all caretaking adults) have their own needs and nightmarish fantasies, conduct to their children their own unconscious terrors, and inadvertently transmit their own intergenerational stories. This applies to parents of cis and non-cis children, of straight and gay children; it is a dynamic, that is, of *all* adult-child dyads.

The issue does not lie in the mother's past and her conflicts, but in the fact that, *for reasons of their own*, the parents cannot abide Ory's translation—which has inventively transformed the mother's difficulties into a version of gender that can be his own. Ory is not, and cannot be, responsible for the parents' distaste for his translation. Part of Ory's burden, however, does involve having to figure out how to live with the fact of their distaste, however unfair to Ory that may be. To put this more bluntly, what Ory has psychically forged out of this intergenerational transmission belongs to him, not to the parents, and for as long as this translation matches his being, it is the analyst's job to help him defend it.

To further clarify, imagine a male-assigned child who manages parental conflicts around perfectionism and self-worth by becoming a skilled football player (doing gender "right"). Such a child would likely get very little pushback and would get to "keep" his gender translation without being constantly surveilled, policed, controlled, rejected, or shamed as Ory is. The formulation we offer, then, is not that Ory has to deal with an inordinate amount of unconscious material vis-à-vis the mother's religio-racial-gender trouble; such psychic matter is always there, especially for families whose social or personal histories are especially burdensome. The critical distinction lies in whether or not children who make something out of that psychic matter are "allowed" to keep their psychic creations, whether they are celebrated for their individualities or treated as "problems" to be "corrected." Translations that accrue to non-normativities are more often met with adult panic, which radiates shame and rejection to the child. In such cases, what is oppressive and, really, tragic is that children as admirable and sturdy as Ory, who has taken his mother's gender trouble and turned it into something robust and beautiful for himself, something that is inspired, lively, and intensely pleasurable, are met by adults in general, and by analysts in particular, with the anxiety of regulation (Corbett 2011). This anxiety and the etiological searches it compels take the beauty and inventiveness of queer life, and much like Ory's orchid, try to "straighten" it and oftentimes squash it. This is how queer children's spirits can be broken. It is this work, the work of dignifying queer individuals' own self-theorizing processes, that we, analysts, owe our patients.

TRAUMA AS RESOURCE

There already is a tradition in psychoanalysis of locating parental psychodynamics at work in the child's atypical gender or homosexual leanings, albeit from a very different angle and with a very different goal (i.e., "correcting" gender atypicality) than what we have been proposing. Consider, for instance, Stoller's early work (1966) arguing that boyhood femininity indexes maternal difficulties with separation, or Coates's suggestion (1990) that boyhood femininity stems from insufficiently mentalized maternal trauma that somehow buckles the child's natural gender trajectory. Motoring a hunt for etiological underpinnings, such quests are shot through with cultural anxiety about regulating proper ways of being a girl or a boy or just a healthy (read: cisheterosexual) human being. Often, the mother is blamed—as was the case with Ilana and as misogyny demands.

We find these theories problematic not because "true" and "authentic" gender is unalloyed by parental conflicts, but because what makes one's gender feel one's own is not its independence from the object, but the freedom to weave together mythosymbolic codes, *including the ones related to the parent's trauma with relative autonomy from the other's control.*[27] We write "relative autonomy" because

---

[27] The reader is reminded that psychoanalytic (cis) gender theory, from Sigmund Freud to Joan Riviere and Robert Stoller, to Ethel Person and Dianne Elise, to Muriel Dimen, Ken Corbett, and Adrienne Harris, to Rosemary Balsam and Jessica Benjamin, has never understood gender to be a solely internally sourced "truth": historically, (cis) genders have always been conceptualized as leaning on or drawing from the relation with one's objects. It is this theoretical and clinical resource that we want to extend to atypically gendered patients.

translations are never entirely independent from the object and its influence, as our discussion of Ory's case illustrates; autonomy refers, rather, to the other (whether the adult, the analyst, the lawmaker, etc.) not trying to exercise control over the child's translational processes.

From this angle, the intergenerational legacy of Ilana's trauma can be seen as inflecting Ory's gender, even serving as a resource for it. Linking intergenerational transmission, trauma, and gender together feels to us like a risky endeavor: trauma can be so easily mobilized to reinforce the current rampant attacks on transness. Beneath atypical genders, this reasoning goes, lie unresolved problems that, if worked through, can "return" the patient to a normative binary position. To be clear, then, we are not suggesting that there might be a way to vacate Ory's feminine presentation, but, to the contrary, we want to underscore that the analyst's ethical responsibility involves not interfering with the patient's translational efforts and their possible outcomes.

This requires psychoanalysis to be able to conceive of homosexuality or transness (just two of the possible paths ahead for Ory) not as failed or unwanted development. We need professional ecosystems in our field that *want* gay people (Sedgwick 1991) and that *want* trans people (Gill-Peterson 2018). In saying this, we are not advocating that analysts try to create non-normative sexual and gender outcomes. Our ethical call is toward metapsychologies and clinical spaces that treat gender and sexual diversity not by simply making room for them or "accepting them,"[28] but by delighting in the pleasures of difference. A proliferation of difference is not a threat but a condition of possibility for enlarged collective living (Preciado 2019).

Hypothesizing that Ory's gender might exist in some complicated relation to his mother's conflict about her own goodness in her family of origin, about her own otherness and the risks that it poses to her own object ties, about what her cis gender "fates" her for in her culture, is not a discovery of what is at the foundations of Ory's gender. What is at stake here is not a question of locus (did it start in him or in her?), which Laplanche describes as an "absurd quarrel over priority" (1998/2017, 193), since the infantile sexual, as we discussed, is always stimulated by and arises in the aftermath of the other's intervention in us. Rather, we may see Ory's gender as a form of translation that fits well enough *for him*—is congruent enough with his own sense of being—*and also* as a way of being that has accommodated an interlock of subject-object dynamics required, it seems, by his mother's history. To the degree that the mother, as we are hypothesizing here, needs her son's gender atypicality to perform a kind of psychic work

28 On the limitations of the rubric of liberal "tolerance" or "acceptance," see Jakobsen and Pellegrini (2004). For a discussion of how the notion of inclusivity—as a mere expansion of who is welcomed in psychoanalysis—fails gender-diverse patients, readers may want to listen to the conversation between Jules Gill-Peterson and Avgi Saketopoulou, on the podcast *Couched*, Episode 5, "Exposing transphobic legacies, embracing trans life" (June 2022).

in the family system that helps locate herself in the center by means of locating him in the margins, her conflicts with her son's otherness deliver her to her family of origin and to her husband as dutiful daughter and wife. Gender trouble is not averted; it has only been passed down to the next generation. But wasn't Ilana's cis gender also some strange tangle between inherited mythosymbolic ideas (about women's duties to religion and family) and her own idiomatic translations? Isn't Ilana, too, in her normative cis gender experience and presentation, also partially a by-product of others' idea of what gender is?

ORCHIDOLOGY

WHERE DOES THAT LEAVE US, clinically speaking, in relation to Ory's gender is or should be?

The clinical task would be extremely complex: to help my (A.S.'s) patient recognize the parental pressures that task him to perform both otherness and compliant normativity, *but to do so without implying that his gender is not his own.* This may be why my comment to him about the bent orchid stem disrupted our work: although on the surface, it was empathetic and compassionate, it also treated Ory's gender not as his own creation, but as "bent" by his mother's neglect. This is not to overlook that her disapproval considerably affected him; it is to note that rather than prioritize his own internal sturdiness—as expressed through his persistent feminine presentation, a noncompliance that he was determined to uphold, a sheer will to be himself rather than wilt under the duress of what was expected of him—my (A.S.'s) comment focused on his injury.

Our position, then, is not that the mother has to process her history so as to "release" her son from the errand he has assumed. Ory was already putting up a fight to be the person he felt he was, whatever form that might take. Consequently, the mother's effort to straighten out the orchid, while clearly of symbolic value in delivering an unambiguous message to Ory, was perhaps not what the treatment should be focused on—as suggested by the fact that my interpretation (A.S.'s) interrupted a nascent momentum in my encounters with Ory. Put differently, Ory was not acting on his mother's unconscious agenda; he very much had his own. To focus on the yes or no of the parent is to question the very foundation of the translation made by the subject, and my interpretation may have made Ory feel more unsteady in the room *with me.* Leaving the treatment was thus part of Ory sturdiness, leaving me wondering what I had done wrong—as well I should. Learning from our mistakes takes humility, because it requires us to admit that we have not served a patient well, but we owe nothing less than such humility to those who come to us for help, especially when we fail them.

Thinking back, we believe that the emphasis might have been better placed on helping Ory continue to claim his gender as his own, rather than noting the possible psychic impact of his mother's suppression of it. If I (A.S.) could rewind time, I would have stayed more with the orchid, the sensuality of its petals, the exquisite attention its care required, and the acute precariousness of its survival. Rather than interpret, I would have waited. It is this kind of waiting that we described earlier in this chapter as *patient affirmation*; the slow time that it involves has to do with slowing down the analyst, not the patient.

The word *orchid*, the *Oxford English Dictionary* explains, comes from the modern Latin *orchis*, which in turn originates in the Greek word όρχης, which means testicle. As a native Greek speaker, this reference was not lost on me (A.S.) during my work with Ory, although I did not yet know how to engage it. There is a plenitude of signifiers here: Ory's testicles as bodily markers of the normative gender his parents wanted him to contort himself to be; as symbolic vehicles of disempowerment in the risks of psychic castration by the other; as speaking to possibilities of unfulfilled homosexual desire; as sites of courage and forcefulness (having the "balls" to be oneself); as metonymically bespeaking and perhaps speaking back to a long history of anti-Semitic stereotypes that "race" and "sex" Jewish difference under the sign of circumcision.

We offer this framework for Ory's case not because we are convinced that the operations we describe are accurate accounts of what *actually* occurred for him or how his gender developed. Rather, we offer our formulations *provisionally,*[29] with the humility of recognizing that, "[l]ike with a dream, one can never reach the 'navel' of gender" (Gozlan in Gozlan et al. 2022, 209). Accordingly, we are less invested in theorizing the origins of Ory's gender and sexuality per se, and more invested in the opportunity this case provides for illustrating a nuanced model of how developmental dynamics, familial history, and intergenerational transmission may bear on gender formation, without that model going "straight." This is not to diminish Ory's suffering, nor the suffering of actual, living children who are routinely subjected to conversion attempts. But we hope that offering a way of thinking about gender constitution through trauma and intergenerational transport may help analysts hold such kids in mind more skillfully than is the norm.

CODA

IN WRITING THIS ACCOUNT, WE struggled with what pronouns to use for Ory. We settled on using he/him pronouns because they were what he used for himself at the time of the treatment.

But we want the reader to know that, even though we feel this was our best choice, we also find it wanting. Queer and trans children oftentimes "grow up sideways"

---

[29] See this volume's preface for the analyst's retrospective reconstructions and why they do not reflect developmental truths.

(Stockton 2009), that is, with their identities deferred until after they reach adulthood. For example, some children who understand themselves to be trans may refrain from calling themselves that because they fear disappointing their primary objects or causing family strife—which could well have been the case with Ory. Thus, even though Ory did not name himself as *trans* at the time of the treatment, it is imaginable that he may grow up to identify as trans and be able to name what will have been his trans childhood only after the fact. Because none of these are (yet?) the case, though, we did not want to choose she/her pronouns for Ory.

In keeping with our wish to sustain an open space for Ory's unfolding gendered possibilities we also gave consideration to using they/them pronouns for him in this chapter. This was not about identifying Ory *with* they/them pronouns or nonbinary gender (again, he used he/him), but to help *the reader* resist the temptation of certainty about Ory's gender now or in the future. We ultimately decided against it, however, because they/them pronouns are also gender specific, affirmatively claimed by many nonbinary and genderqueer individuals. Instead of marking and holding a not-yet-determined outcome, then, using they/them would risk implying that we already know Ory will come to identify as nonbinary, when in fact we know no such thing.

The space we have labored to hold is this: neither of us knows who Ory will grow up to be, how his gender may congeal, and whether or how it will shapeshift with time. We would not be surprised if Ory comes to identify as gay, as trans, as nonbinary, if he settles into he/him/his pronouns, or into some other gender form we cannot yet imagine. Nor do we know if he will remain within his religious world, or if he will go "off the *derech*," that is, off the path, and leave his religious community.[30] It is not for us to play prophet and decide the question of who or what Ory will become. Neither, dear reader, should you.

---

[30] *Off the derech* may seem like a pejorative but, in fact, many individuals who have left their Orthodox communities have taken on the label *OTD* as a point of affirmation. (For more on this, the interested reader can consult Cappell and Lang [2020] and Naomi Seidman's podcast *Heretic in the House* [2022].)

2

ON TAKING SIDES: CLINICAL ENCOUNTERS WITH NONBINARY GENDERS[1]

We cannot organize...our individual identities and desires without...[categories]. The fact that these categories invariably leak and can never contain all the relevant "existing things" does not render them useless, only limited. Categories like "woman," "butch," "lesbian," or "transsexual" are all imperfect, historical, temporary, and arbitrary. We use them, and they use us.

—Gayle Rubin, "Of Catamites and Kings: Reflections on Butch, Gender, and Boundaries"

Do we force a choice in the form of *he, she,* or, if they're generous *they*; or do we take whatever is offered, letting it slowly cultivate the texture of another kind of world?

—Marquis Bey, "Re: [No Subject]—On Nonbinary Gender"

---
[1] An earlier version of this chapter was published, in June 2019, by *Psychoanalysis.today* (see Pellegrini and Saketopoulou, 2019.)

After much layered psychoanalytic work, your 30-year-old patient Kyle announces, with some anxiety if not trepidation, their decision to change gender pronouns. Kyle has been moving toward a gender they describe as nonbinary. They are now ready, they say, to switch to using *they/them* to refer to themselves and plan to ask others to do the same. Kyle makes explicit that those others include you, their analyst. You are asked to follow suit. You are asked, we might say, to take sides.

How are you, their analyst, to understand such a request? Or more precisely, what is it that you are being asked to side with?

Psychoanalysis has struggled with how to understand gender transitions in the context of transgender patients. But just as we try to contend seriously with trans experience and embodiment (Gherovici 2017; Gozlan 2019; Hansbury 2011; Harris 2009; Langer 2016; Pula 2015; Saketopoulou 2014; Silverman 2016)—a beginning that finds us both outpaced and out of breath—the gender horizon seems to recede yet again. Beyond the presumed ideality of a full transition that starts in one gender (the gender of assignment) and has a clear, coherent, and identifiable gender destination (the gender of identification/ arrival) lies a cornucopia of genders. These wildly plural genders are strange in the most elemental meaning of the word: they are strangers, outsiders, seemingly foreign to the world of cis gender, a world that is itself a fantasized construction—albeit one propped up with considerable social force.

The term *cisgender* is a neologism that dates to 1994 and that trans studies scholar Finn Enke credits to biologist Dana Leland Defosse (Enke 2012). In its early usages within trans activist communities, cisgender offered an "analytic of the unseen privilege and power of a set of common assumptions: that gender was visible and obvious, that sex was immutable, and that gender was a natural biological expression of sex" (Amin 2022, 109). But words shapeshift, and some time around 2008, Enke noticed that his undergraduate students were using *cisgender* in new ways: as an identity category for anyone who was non-trans.

As the name for an identity, *cis* came to signify the (ostensibly natural) alignment between gender assignment and gender experience. Because this fiction is also socially dominant, cisness is buffered by all manner of supports and reinforcements such that cis genders can come to appear effortless, natural, the way things are and are supposed to be. But such a conception misses the labor required to translate and elaborate *any* gender, including cis gender formations. In other words, cis genders are not expectable, natural genders: they too are genders that coagulate into a sense of self through considerable translational psychic work. That this psychic work is rendered invisible by virtue of its normativity does not mean that such labor does not exist, only that it is not easily apparent.

It is important not to underestimate the punitive

force with which gender norms are imposed even on those bodies and subjects who understand, could understand, or are pressured to understand themselves to be "cis." "I surely was not born this way," writes Marquis Bey, "which is to say on this side, cis, etymologically. I was very deliberately, very meticulously, crafted through violent means to remain on this side" (2022, 18). More proximally to psychoanalysis, think about Joan Riviere, whose early essay "Womanliness as a Masquerade" (1929) described the toil, anguish, and interpersonal constraint that gives "womanliness" its density. Cisness is thus less a naturally occurring identity (which transness and nonbinary genders stray from or oppose) than it is a description of a compulsory system "that *demands* a match between anatomy and identity" (Gill-Peterson 2021, italics added).

When the match this compulsory system demands is not delivered, one is exacted anyway, and clinical experience shows time and again how violently scarred such "cisgender" patients' psyches can be. We put *cisgender* in quotations here to indicate how scorching it can be to be disciplined into normative gender, to learn to produce (for others, sometimes even for oneself) a cisness that is undergirded by suppression, at times dissociatively. In "The Masculine Vaginal," Griffin Hansbury coined the term *vaginal castration* to capture the fate of cis-identified men "who, as boys, did not conform to gender norms and were thus subjected to vigorous and sometimes violent gender policing" (2017, 1022).

Similar violences are, of course, perpetrated against "cis" girls who are implored, pressured, and shamed into producing versions of femininities that do not match their being, and that require them to splice their activity, ambition, initiative. The idea that cisgender boys are not only methodically denied a sense of psychic interiority, but are also unsparingly pressured to neutralize their passive and receptive elements because they assail what cis masculinity is supposed to be, underlines that the category of cisness is neither spontaneous nor the default, and that it requires a level of violence and dissociation for its maintenance (Corbett 2007; Goldner 2011; Salamon 2018).

Atypical genders expose those who think of themselves as "gender normal" (as many cis-analysts do) to gendered concoctions that may strain thinking. We are reminded of a normatively gendered child patient who poignantly described her reaction to an atypically gendered peer, protesting that her schoolmate "makes my brain hurt" (Saketopoulou 2011, 205). It is in the nature of immature psychic defenses to attribute to the other the hurting of one's own brain, a strain that arises when confronted with difference one cannot psychically bear. Analysts who become curious about their own brain-hurt have a better chance at working well with genderqueer patients. We use the term *cis-analyst* here not to designate an identity, as in an analyst who *identifies as* cis gender, but as a critical shorthand to highlight the "pass" conferred by "sex/gender congruence, legibility, and consistency within a binary gender system…, particularly when accompanied by the appearance of normative race, class, ability, and nationality" (Enke 2012, 64). Gender normativity thus surfaces—*and is surfaced by*—other norms, such as whiteness and able-bodiedness.

A critically queer disability studies lens is helpful here. Writing about her changed life and embodiment after being paralyzed in a bicycling accident, Christina Crosby powerfully distills the cross-hatching of norms of gender and physical capacity: "I no longer have a gender. Rather, I have a wheelchair" (2016, 60). Absorbed into what she calls the "gestalt" of the wheelchair, her "butchy" way of doing her lesbian body before her accident no longer scanned; post-accident she found herself being "misrecognized as a man" with much greater frequency than before (2016, 60), a misgendering she experienced as a de-sexing and un-gendering. For Crosby, un-gendering was linked to the hypervisibility of her disability.

But un-gendering also has implications in the domain of race and racialization. A powerful tradition in Black feminist theory examines the violent stripping away of subjectivity under slavery as captive bodies were turned into raw and commodified flesh. This "mutilation," Hortense Spillers writes, was also a stripping away of "*gender* difference in the outcome" (1987, 67, emphasis in original). Gendered personhood, in this reckoning, is one of the properties of whiteness. The co-constitution of norms of whiteness and binary gender place Black subjects and other people of color beyond the pale of cisness, because "racialization muddies cisgender identity" (Bey 2022, 24). But this very same predicament—of being denied normative privilege—may also make nonbinary gender appear to be "a privilege only afforded those proximal to whiteness, since nonbinariness is believed to be possessed only by those not subject to needing gender as a vector through which to gain personhood, the case for many people of color" (Bey 2021, 231).

Nevertheless, it is certainly the case that many people, including many analysts, do self-consciously identify themselves as cisgender, often as a form of trans allyship to display their awareness of their privileges (Enke 2012, 62). While recognizing the gestural and political significance of such a move, however, along with other trans, queer, and feminist scholars, we are concerned about the ways the prefixes *trans* and *cis* may too quickly get turned into fixed and opposed identities through this very gesture of allyship.[2]

For cis analysts, the encounter with gender diverse patients can bring up feelings of unfamiliarity, surprise, and other affects that may defensively mutate into the formulation that such genders are idiosyncratic oddities, eccentric concoctions that seek to accommodate

---

[2] For more on these concerns, see the preface to this volume, and the distinction between being an ally versus being an accomplice.

pathological narcissism and other deviations. Unusual gender forms that do not contort themselves around cis male/cis female presentations, but dart instead to and from masculinity and femininity, may thus be met by the analyst with bewilderment, incredulity, even anger. Not infrequently, nonbinary genders may revivify in cis clinicians the dissociations and repressions keeping their own cis experience in place, arousing affects that remained in the psychic background till brought forth in the encounter with a nonbinary patient. It is obvious that such anxieties need the analyst's tending and attention. When they go unprocessed, the analyst may become strangely controlling or sadistic (Hansbury 2017) or experience a primitive kind of gender terror, a condition of feeling destabilized in both specific and nonspecific ways. All these reactions can obviously interfere with the clinician's ordinary capacity to wait for material to emerge, to reflect on her countertransference, and to allow the unexpected to unfold without trying to master the turbulence it generates in the room.

It is worth noting that the encounter between cis clinicians and variantly gendered patients can feel challenging to the expansive theoretical efforts of colleagues who see themselves as more open-minded because they are willing to "concede" that some patients are better off transitioning (see, e.g., Lemma 2018). Indeed, a growing number of analysts are starting to recognize that social and medical transitioning may be a viable psychic option for some patients (rather than a concretization of psychotic operations [Chiland 2000; Kubie 1974]). That makes it possible for psychoanalysis to imagine good adaptations for patients seeking full transitions (Gherovici 2017). But otherwise complex genders, such as nonbinary ones, are harder to address with similar sensitivity and imaginative capacity in our analytic literature, leading colleagues to reach for simplistic, non-analytic overgeneralizations and formulations that are both panic-driven and panic-inducing: for example, the transphobic idea that one can "catch" atypical gender on the internet (Bell 2020) or that gender diversity is "an epidemic" comparable to that of the opioid crisis (Evans and Evans 2021, 217) to which female-assigned and gay children are particularly vulnerable (D'Angelo 2020).

What, however, is nonbinary gender?

Briefly, the term pertains to a wide array of gender constitutions and embodied possibilities. Unlike some other categories of gender polymorphism, it does not have fixed referents, making nonbinary gender impossible to theorize as a singular category.[3] Nonbinary gender does not anchor itself in assigned sex, does not point toward a final destination, and does not aim toward a cohesive gender presentation. If the subject's presentation does, at some point, end up reading male or female, it may do so

---

[3]   This is not to suggest that normative genders, trans femininities, or trans masculinities are easily classifiable under the aegis of any single term.

ironically, perhaps with an element of camp (Sontag 1964). Additionally, not all nonbinary people want or choose medical interventions. Those who do may not approach gendered embodiment as a matter of aligning bodily morphology to gender identity—as is usually the case with full transition. Instead, they may treat their gendered body as inhabiting multiple, distinct zones that don't have to cohere into a unified presentation. For example, someone assigned female at birth (AFAB), and identifying as gender nonbinary or trans nonbinary, may opt for top surgery but not seek androgenizing treatments. Another nonbinary AFAB person may use hormones with an eye toward modulating or blurring masculinizing effects.

Recently, *nonbinary* has become even blurrier, harder to pin down. While initially, Kadji Amin provocatively observes, nonbinary "offered a much-needed home to all those orphans at the fuzzy edges of the cis/trans binary…, nonbinary identity is [increasingly] being claimed by people who look and behave in a manner indistinguishable from ordinary lesbians and gays, or even ordinary heterosexuals" (2022, 113). What accounts for this differently employed rise in nonbinary identification, he suggests, is that nonbinary identity offers a (Western-based) resistance to the fantasized naturalness and coherence of cis identity. It is a shorthand, in other words, for those who have no interest in transitioning but who find that their projects of self-theorizations are not sufficiently captured by the terms *man* or *woman*.

As psychoanalysts, we are easily challenged by this mix-and-match aspect of nonbinary genders because we are trained to think of bodies as needing to function as integrated, coherent wholes. Consequently, a body not ordered around cis male or cis female embodiment is easily seen as a *de facto* manifestation of psychic fragmentation. But gender is not the only way to organize and "cohere" the body. Psychoanalysis, in fact, is exquisitely equipped to illuminate other avenues by which the body can be organized and inhabited—sexuality being one of them. This is not to say that nonbinary genders are not propelled by psychic processes, or that they do not fall under the aegis of the sexual drives. Quite the contrary: no psychic operation, including gender, normative or not, operates outside the domain of the sexual unconscious. What we are arguing instead is that nonbinary genders are idiosyncratic assemblages that need their own unpacking and, in the consulting room, require time and patience for their elaboration.

Psychoanalytic treatments have much to contribute toward such endeavors, as long as we appreciate what Laplanche explains about gender assignment: that the phallic logic on which it has relied (that is, the visual inspection of the genital area at birth) has been binary, used to "assign [people] to two groups…male and female" (Laplanche et al. 2000, 37). This logic, he continues, is inhumane, akin to the one "used in computers…zero and one, yes and no, the presence or absence of a single attribute" (ibid.). The subject is always left having to "treat" the message of this binary gender assignment, as well as to "treat" the enigmatic surpluses that inevitably compromise it, to find ways of "elaborating, of treating the question of [one's] gender" (ibid.).

Indeed, this is one generative way to understand the patient Kyle's request. Although Kyle speaks as if they are in possession of some final knowledge about their gender, our clinical experience suggests that patients like Kyle may be best thought of as having embarked on auto-poietic projects that treat enigma through gender categories, both those given to the subject and those creatively expanded by them. To take sides, then, is to side with the autonomy of the subject's auto-theorizing process (Laplanche 1987). What the analyst joins is the patient's effort to see whether these self-creations, whatever they may be, can "take." What the work of analysis can offer is to sustain the patient as they labor through them—for example, by exploring whether addressing dynamic issues and tackling anxiety and defense can clear the path for the subject to be able to thrive, and even bolster their self-theorizations. It is also the analyst's responsibility to be there for the patient, for those occasions that their self-theorizing projects may fail, as the patient agonizingly embarks on new vistas of self-making—which is one way to think about de-transitioning and re-transitioning.

The reader may have noticed that, again, we are not speaking about the accuracy of the patient's efforts, about whether it accords with some objective truth, nor are we looking to ascertain whether it draws on sources that make sense to the analyst (e.g., identifications with the primary objects as opposed to trauma). We advocate for the analyst's maintaining a respectful but mindful distance from the patient's process, in touch with her own enigma, and attuned to how her own sexual unconscious participates in provoking the transference (Laplanche 2011; Scarfone 2010), which is how the analytic process always unfurls. Sometimes the process has to start not with reflection, but with action on the patient's part—in this case, the act of pronouncing oneself to be nonbinary, requesting a shift in pronouns, or embarking on the experiment of hormone therapy. But in this model, such action is not necessarily a problem, nor is it a challenge to the therapeutic endeavor. And if the word *experiment* makes you anxious, let us remind you that every time a patient treads into new territory, the process is experimental, which does not mean that it is to be taken lightly or nonchalantly, but that it opens up the patient—and to a certain degree, the analyst too—to uncertain, unpredictable effects.

In contrast, then, to those who would argue that the analyst should delay Kyle's request for they/them pronouns until the dyad first explores the meanings and terms of that request, we opt for a both/and position. Acceding to Kyle's request becomes a way of facilitating their exploration, their testing of whether their self-theorization can work, whether it can acquire the depth and sustain the density of who they understand themselves to be or who they are trying to become. We see it as the *analyst's* job to hold time and space for Kyle to work on the dynamic process that underlies what gender means to them as Kyle uses nonbinary gender to treat enigma, and finds themselves drawing on archives as rich and diverse as intergenerationally transmitted traumata, parental anxieties, social prescriptions and proscriptions to translate autonomously. All this is to be held in the analyst's mind but *without the analyst's intrusion.*

This also means that it is not Kyle's responsibility to lucidly and convincingly articulate themselves to their analyst before such work can proceed. It is not just that such articulations are often and only arrived at in the après-coup, but also that the analyst needs to bear the complexities of nonlinear, scrambled time, which is necessary but not at all easy. This process oftentimes involves a willingness on the analyst's part to take a leap, to explore with the patient what may become possible around their patient's experimentation with their gender—a domain of self-experimentation that many colleagues feel uncomfortable with.

In such endeavors, uncertainty reigns for both analyst and patient, and its coordinates are not possible to plot ahead of time. This "uncertainty," Bey poignantly writes, is about "wanting *that* without knowing what *that* will be, but understanding it as an anarchic salvation precisely because it is not *this*" (Bey 2020a, 42, italics in original).

Such inscrutability is neither an attack on the work nor a refusal of a relation with the analyst, but a rewriting of the terms by which a therapeutic relation can be sustained and flourish; not necessarily a withholding or a pushing the analyst away, but an invitation to a different kind of encounter. The analyst, in other words, need not feel anxious that such taking of sides involves a collusion with something destructive or problematic, even as pain and anguish may well prove to be part of the process for the patient.

"Negative affects do much more than chip away at one's ability to get by (though they certainly *do* do that)," Malatino writes emphatically (2022, 17, italics in original). They can also make things possible, provide unforeseen openings and forge new opportunities. What work may be possible if we analysts become less controllingly protectionist of gender-diverse patients and less invested in our need to safeguard the patient from imagined harms that intensely preoccupy *us*?

Without a doubt, as analysts, we are always mindful of the numerous implications in being asked by patients, implicitly or explicitly, to take sides. Relational psychoanalytic thinking has long alerted us to the fantasy that there is a way to sidestep this; refusing to take sides is just the taking of a(n other) side (Aron 2001; Aron and Starr 2013). Refusing to use they/them pronouns is thus not a neutral act either—unless one uncritically adopts the perspective that Kyle's gender is known and that the analyst is being asked to become complicit with its distortion, a perspective we have been urging analysts to question. In agreeing or disagreeing with Kyle's request, the analyst necessarily tips her hand. "Pronouns," Bey argues, "are like tiny vessels of verification that others are picking up what you are putting down" (2021, 238). What you, Kyle's analyst, are being asked to verify is not the truth of gender's final destination. Rather, in picking up what Kyle put in the space before you, you mark the "yes" of your interest, the "yes" of a curiosity without bannisters, the "yes" of "I will embark on this adventure with you."

To say this differently, we are not proposing that adopting the patient's pronouns is "neutral." The analyst's infantile sexual will always inflect her communicative acts (be they verbal or nonverbal), compromising (in the Laplanchean sense) her communications about being willing to embark on the patient's voyage. An encounter with a non-normatively gendered patient may well unsettle a cis analyst's own foreclosed, identity-bound infantile sexuality (Hansbury and Saketopoulou 2022), and we would expect this to be especially the case for analysts who have psychically organized themselves through tighter gender/sexual bindings—as, for instance, analysts whose own gender identity is rigidly bound or mostly uninterrogated. We emphasize that neither position is neutral not because we subscribe to the notion that "neutrality" is an ideal clinical stance (we don't), but because we want to remind our colleagues that whatever one's conscious, considered reasoning may be regarding the patient's request that we take sides, there is no sidestepping the fact that our stance will be inflected by our own sexual unconscious, which will, in turn, affect how the patient's transference takes shape.

For the purposes of thinking about patients like Kyle, and about nonbinary genders and they/them pronouns more generally, we want to stress that the issue is not a matter of taking sides with a particular gender outcome (i.e., the analyst "accepting" Kyle's gender), but of taking seriously that what is at stake is the patient's processual and future unspooling. Oftentimes, the patient announces a pronoun change as a fait accompli. In doing so, they are also trying to craft a space for self-definition of something that would feel solid to them. That space may or may not shift during the course of the analysis: in other words, it has to feel solid, but that does not mean that it will (or has to) remain so. We would all agree that Kyle's need and growing capacity to stake such a claim deserves our analytic attention, but rather than focus on the claim's *content* per se, an analyst might be better off prioritizing the patient's *effort* to craft new meanings about themselves. We often see a hot-potato-in-the-room situation when the analyst thinks the patient is being "too concrete" and won't keep gender hybridity where it is said to belong: in the realm of fantasy or psychic bisexuality (D'Angelo 2021; Evans and Evans 2021).

But what if it is the analyst who is becoming overly

concrete in narrowing her sights and refusing to join the patient in exploration? To remain vibrantly curious, the analyst will need to interrogate her own concreteness, her own wish to stabilize herself by holding onto the familiar, perhaps even her refusal to sit with the disturbance that her patient's gender or embodiment is bringing to the analyst's infantile sexuality and to her own gender experience (see, e.g., Quinodoz 1998; Silverman 2023; Suchet 2011).

In many cases, the patient's process of gender-becoming is set in motion by the analytic encounter: the reestablishment of a space where "the *essence* of the primal" is put "back into play" (Laplanche 1987, 180, italics in original), unsettling previous translations, which, in turn, unleashes psychic energies that may kindle new theorizations in the patient. What a paradox, then, that in some cases, the very processes by which something opens up in the patient may panic the analyst.

The trans-identified psychoanalyst Jack Pula offers a striking example of exactly such a thing occurring in his first analysis, which he writes about in his 2015 autobiographical essay. Pula describes how it was through his treatment that he "came into my manhood, not just in my mind, and not just as an analytic artifact or enactment. I found the toddler boy buried deep inside who longed to sit in my analyst's lap and be snuggled and kissed. I found the hesitant child giggling for approval….I became emboldened by felt urges in my sexed and gendered body, genital feelings and longings, in addition to a multitude of other gendered body feelings that brought delight and glimpses of affective liberty" (2015, 814). In Pula's treatment, "use of the couch, frequency of sessions, lack of eye contact, and ripe transference—[all] cherished facilitators of psychoanalysis—finally allowed me to access my body as a transgender person" (813). But rather than Pula's analyst welcoming these transformations and holding space for curiosity about this unexpected turn that the analysis itself motored, Pula's gender shifts resulted in an irresolvable impasse. The work had to be terminated. "As I continue my psychoanalytic training and my transition," Pula notes poignantly, "I remain haunted by that first analysis and its derailment" (814).

Pula identifies as trans, not as nonbinary, but his set of reflections powerfully illustrates how gender identification may expansively shift in the course of, *and because of,* an analysis. But it also shows how this opening is not always bearable *to the analyst* and how much pain the patient feels at the analyst's refusal to engage with what the analysis itself has facilitated. Our supervisory experience has shown us that such an analyst's panicked response may arise from the analyst's inability to tolerate that the impact of the treatment is so spectacularly powerful that it can enable such monumental shifts. Wherever that response may come from, however, it can create a dreadfully difficult situation for the patient whose newfound singularity is met with little support, and even covert hostility. Here is Pula again, painfully reflecting on his experience through the lens of his second analysis: "I am convinced," he writes, that "it was harmful for me to lose the continuity of my [first] treatment at a time when it could have been so transformative" (2015, 814).

So, returning to thinking about the shift toward nonbinary genders, what if our task is not to explore what a request for a pronoun shift means—a focus that privileges represented, even if disguised or repressed, meanings—but to attend to what this new form of address may enable, what future hatchings it may permit? We don't yet know, nor does Kyle, who or how they will become through the trying on of this new pronoun—as they speak it and think it, and as others speak it and think it of them, as it flushes their body and as it inflects their desire. Gender is not a private language; it requires at least two parties and is embroiled in entire lifeworlds and world orders. Gender implicates us with others, makes us vulnerable to their address, to the ways they do and do not call our names, the ways they do and do not hold us in mind, the ways they do and do not lust after us. In the face-to-face of the dyad, there is scant occasion for the analyst to refer to the patient in the third person. The pronouns exchanged between them are more commonly the direct address of *I* and *you*. The announcement by patient to analyst—"I want to be called 'they'" —thus does not necessarily express something straightforward, but perhaps indicates the hope to be held in mind under this new name beyond the beat of the 45-minute hour (Pellegrini, in Garfinkle et al. 2019, 687).

In this regard, Kyle's decision does not close down possibility; it makes a claim for something still very much in process, something that may only after the fact be revealed to be about Kyle's future becoming (Muñoz 2009). What an honor to be invited by a patient to be part of something yet unknown, to be trusted to accompany the patient in a journey with uncertain destinations, to court the emergence of something new, alien, and strange, to watch the patient try something on, even if it is later to be discarded, even if it becomes undone, gets redone, or is found to have been overdone and needs to be done over. It is easy under such conditions of uncertainty, and with patients in transient states of *becoming*, for the analyst to find herself impatient, anxious, perturbed, and even paranoid in the face of analysands who are not just challenging the gender binary,[4] but who also bend the grammars of gendered subjectivity as well as protocols of psychoanalytic diagnosis. Without a distinct and discernible symptom to hold onto, the analyst may decide that the gender being declared, customized, and enacted *is* the symptom. What would it take for analysts to be able to marvel at such invitations rather than become drenched in anxiety? How might we foster the sturdiness that would

---

[4] Many versions of trans also challenge the gender binary, as do many feminist deconstructions of gender stereotypes. We are not arguing that nonbinary genders are exclusively capable of such challenges, nor that their underlying motivation is (only) to mess with gender dualities.

be required in ourselves and in our colleagues to meet our patients' sturdiness?

At minimum, we often hear the muted protest that *they* is grammatically incorrect—and that expecting the analyst to use an odd locution is a constraint on her freedom to think and dream the patient. But this is only true in the anxious analyst's mind; yes, *they* is not common as a singular pronoun, but in English, *they/them/theirs* are not so much new gender pronouns as they are *renewed* ones. The use of *they* as a singular pronoun has a much earlier history, with attested uses as early as 1315 and well into the eighteenth century (Baron 2018). Besides, English speakers routinely rely on *they* when referring to a person whose gender is unknown (as in: "my daughter's doctor prescribed medication; *they* think it might help"). This is all to say that language changes, and so do gendered possibilities—though not always in sync with each other. The ongoing mutation of language and categories is no trivial matter, as evidenced by fiery political debates over gender pronouns in the United States (and elsewhere). Some seem to worry that gender itself is being destroyed, a claim that quickly assumes cosmic proportions, as if the pronoun *they* can cancel out natural and divine orders at once.[5]

---

[5] We see this ratcheting up in the Vatican's recent attack on "gender theory" for questioning the "reciprocity and complementarity of male-female relationships, [and] the procreative end of sexuality" (Versaldi 2019).

We also hear of analysts who feel that their mind and reality are under attack when asked to use new gender pronouns to refer to and think about a patient (D'Angelo 2020). Such an analyst is not entirely wrong; they aren't just being paranoid. There is indeed a challenge, though not one mounted by a particular patient against a specific analyst; paranoia may set in as a hypertrophied response to radical challenges to cis normativity and to the way it orders the world. The world as "we" know it is giving way to new forms—in the clinic and beyond. To many of our colleagues, this can indeed feel vertiginous, the ground shifting beneath couch and chair, but it is not necessarily a problem, except for those who believe in worlds that remain unchanging and who are unprepared to work with the unexpected.

The struggle of psychoanalysis to keep pace with changing possibilities of gender and embodiment is taking place against the backdrop of contentious and often violent debates in the wider public. The difficulties and anxieties some analysts may have are thus not theirs alone. But it is also our strong hope that psychoanalysis can live up to the challenge of making the world bigger and more livable for the "wild profusion of existing" genders (Foucault 1970; Rubin 1992). And for those yet to come.

3

GENDER, SEX AND THE *SEXUAL*[1]
Jean Laplanche

<u>Gender</u> *is plural. It is ordinarily double, as in masculine-feminine, but it is not so by nature. It is often plural, as in the history of languages, and in social evolution.*

<u>Sex</u> *is dual. It is so by virtue of sexual reproduction and also by virtue of its human symbolization, which sets and freezes the duality as presence/absence, phallic/castrated.*

The <u>sexual</u> *is multiple, polymorphous. The fundamental discovery of Freud, it is based on repression, the unconscious, and fantasy. It is the object of psychoanalysis.*[2]

[1] First published in *Libres cahiers pour la psychanalyse. Études sur la Théorie de la séduction* (Paris: In Press, 2003), pp. 69–103. This English translation, by Jonathan House, first appeared as chapter nine of *Freud and the <u>Sexual</u>* (2011, 159-201).

[2] [*Unconscious in Translation (UIT) Editor*: Laplanche invents a neologism in French by transforming the German component adjective *Sexual-* into a free-standing noun, in pointed contrast with the standard French term *sexuel*. (In German *Sexual* mainly appears as a bound adjectival root in combination with a noun, e.g. *Sexualtrieb*—sexual drive, *Sexualtheorie*—sexual theory). This is an attempt to register terminologically the difference between the enlarged Freudian notion of sexuality (*le sexual*) and the common sense or traditional notion of a genital sexuality (*le sexuel*). This terminological innovation can't really be captured in English as the German term *Sexual* coincides exactly with the spelling of the standard English term "sexual," rather than contrasting with it as in French. The translators have chosen to signal Laplanche's neologism by italicizing *sexual*—pronounced with a long "a": *ahl*.]

Proposition: The sexual is the unconscious residue of the symbolization-repression of gender by sex.

WHAT I PRESENT HERE IS a sort of synthesis—one which is too abbreviated and which merits further development—of a work that we have pursued for about three years in my teaching and research seminar; the basic question being, to put things in a very classical manner, the question of sexual identity—as it is called in psychoanalysis.

The current tendency is to speak of gender identity, and the question immediately arises whether this is simply a change in vocabulary or something more profound. Is it a positive development or the mark of a repression, and if there is repression, where is it? As you may know, I tend to think that "repression in theory" and "repression in the thing itself"—that is to say in the concrete evolution of the individual—often go hand in hand.

My plan will be very simple. First, I shall spend a little time on conceptual distinctions and on the question, "why introduce gender?" and then, for the second part, I shall sketch the functioning, in the early history of the human being, of the triad gender—sex—*sexual*.

*

* *

CONCEPTUAL DISTINCTIONS ARE NOT WORTHWHILE in themselves but only for the conflictual potentialities they harbour; if they are binary they are often the mark of negation and therefore of repression. Some displacements may hide repressions. So it is with the displacement of the question of sexual identity onto the question of gender identity. What this displacement perhaps conceals is that the fundamental Freudian discovery does not lie in gender identity but—besides gender, besides sex or the sexed—in the question of the *sexual*.

Following Freud, I would like to distinguish between the sexual (*le sexuel*) and the sexed (*le sexué*) or that which concerns "sex." It has been claimed, perhaps correctly, that the etymology of "sex" is from "…cut," because the "sexed" clearly entails the *difference* of the sexes or the *difference* of sex, which in German is called an "*Unterschied*."[3] There is the "*sexual*," for example, in "The Three Essays on *Sexualtheorie*," that is to say on the theory of the sexual (*le sexuel*) or rather what I would call "the *sexual* (*le sexual*)." It is perhaps an eccentricity on my part to speak of *le sexual* and not *le sexuel*, but I do so in order to indicate clearly this opposition and the originality of the Freudian concept.[4] In German, there are two terms. There is "*Geschlecht*," of

[3] In a quite general way, although not systematically, Freud uses the term *Unterschied* (difference) to indicate a binary opposition and *Verschiedenheit* (diversity) when there is a plurality of terms: difference between black and white, diversity of colours. [*UIT Editor*: cf. "18th December, 1973, Laplanche, 1980", 44-58].

[4] In German the derivation of the terms *sexuell* and *sexual* is very close. The provenance of both is the Latin *sexualis*. "Sexual" is more erudite and more Germanic; "sexuell" has more a flavour of the Romance languages and has more common currency.

course, which means "sexed sex," but there is also "*Sexual*," the sexual (*le sexuel*), which I am calling the "*le sexual*." When Freud speaks of enlarged sexuality, the sexuality of the *Three Essays*, it is always the *sexual*. It would have been unthinkable for Freud to have entitled his inaugural work, "Three Essays on the Theory of the Sexed—or of Sexuation." "*Sexualtheorie*" is not a "*Geschlechtstheorie*."[5] It is a sexuality that has been called "non-procreative" and even primarily non-sexed, as distinct from what is called precisely "sexed reproduction." The *sexual*, then, is not the sexed; it is essentially perverse infantile sexuality.

"Enlarged" sexuality is the great psychoanalytic discovery, maintained from beginning to end and difficult to conceptualize—as Freud himself shows when he tries to reflect on the question in, for example, his *Introductory Lectures*. It is infantile, certainly, more closely connected to fantasy than to the object, and is thus auto-erotic, governed by fantasy, governed by the unconscious. (Isn't the unconscious ultimately the *sexual*? One can legitimately ask this question). So for Freud, the "*sexual*" is exterior to, even prior to, the difference of the sexes, even the difference of the genders: it is oral, anal or para-genital.

Nevertheless, whenever Freud tries to define it he is

---

[5]   Conversely, Freud employs the term *Geschlechtlichkeit* in a quite specific sense, different from that of "sexuality." This is the case in *The Interpretation of Dreams* (1900) where there is "a conversation in which 'it was just as though we had become aware of our *sex*, it was as though I were to say: 'I'm a man and you're a woman'" (333).

brought back to the need to put it into relation with what it is not, that is to say, with sexed activity or with sex; and he does this according to the three classic paths of the association of ideas. First, the path of *resemblance*: Freud seeks resemblances between the pleasures of the *sexual*, the pleasures of infantile sexuality or perverse pleasures, and what is characteristic of genital sexuality, namely the experience of orgasm. Some of the resemblances are more or less valid; some are more or less artificial, such as that claimed between the "blissful smile" of the sated nursling and "the expression of sexual satisfaction in later life" (Freud 1905, 182). Second and above all, there are the arguments of *contiguity*: contiguity since the *sexual* is found in foreplay and in the perversions contiguous to genital orgasm; and even the argument of "anatomical" contiguity, which Freud already calls a sort of "destiny," in which the contiguity is between the vagina and the rectum (Freud 1912, 189, 187n).

But what I would like to stress instead is association "by *opposition*," which among the associationists is typically referred to as the "third type of association." Does *sexual* pleasure exist in *opposition* to sexed pleasure? Doubtless this is often true in reality, in the pursuit of erotic activities, even in terms of economic characteristics, since one may imagine—I shall perhaps return to this—that the economic functioning of the "*sexual*" is aimed at the pursuit of tension, whereas the "sexed" aims rather at the classic pleasure of relaxation. But this is not the true opposition. We encounter a sort of subversion of the very notion of logical opposition, which itself suddenly becomes an opposition in the real, i.e. a prohibition. In other words, the *sexual* is defined as "that which is condemned by the adult." There is not a single text by Freud in which he speaks of infantile sexuality without putting this opposition forward, not as a sort of contingent reaction to infantile sexuality, but as something that truly *defines* it. I believe that even these days infantile sexuality, strictly speaking, is what is most repugnant in the eyes of the adult. Even today "bad habits" remain the most difficult thing for adults to accept. So it is a curious definition, by opposition. By a sort of circular reasoning the sexual is condemned because it is sexual, but it is sexual, or "*sexual*," because it is condemned. The *sexual* is the repressed; it is repressed because it is the *sexual*.

Here, then, we confront the great difficulty of having to define an enlarged sexuality that we appear to be able to grasp only in terms of its relation to what is sexed, to sexuality in the classic sense. Will introducing a third term save us, or will it rather add to the confusion, add to the repression?

The third term is "gender," which was first introduced in English, but which came to be translated or transposed into different languages and in particular into French. The notion of gender is currently enjoying such success among sociologists, feminists, and especially among feminist sociologists, that it is supposed to have been introduced by them. In fact, it is now established that the term was introduced by the sexologist John Money in 1955, and later reintroduced, with well-known success, by Robert Stoller, who in 1968 created the term "core gender identity." He thus integrated the term into specifically psychoanalytic thought.[6]

Here it would be necessary to enter into the infinite and powerfully seductive variations of Stoller's thought—a non-conventional thinker who is very interesting even if he often contradicts himself. I particularly like to cite what he says about contemporary psychoanalytic thought when he compares it to the Pantheon of imperial Rome, where temples to the most diverse divinities coexisted in a kind of joyous jumble (Stoller 1985, 82).

However, my main argument is that with Stoller, and after him, the notion of gender becomes a synonym for a set of convictions: the conviction of belonging to one of two social groups defined as masculine or feminine, or else the conviction that the assignment to one of these two groups is correct. I shall come back to this term "assignment."

I shall not follow Stoller's thinking here.[7] What

GENDER WITHOUT IDENTITY

---

6 Robert Stoller, *Sex and Gender* (London: The Hogarth Press, 1968), which was published in a French translation under the title *Recherches sur l'identité sexuelle* (Paris: Gallimard, 1978). The transposition of the title alone shows the difficulty classical French psychoanalytic thought has in integrating the term and the idea of gender.

7 Cf. "Appendix I: Stoller and Gender."

interests me is the appearance of this new anglophone binary, the sex-gender couple. "Sex" being understood principally as biological, and "gender" as socio-cultural but also as subjective. The problem thus arises of the politics of translation into languages with no common usage of the word "gender." French more or less had this, but mainly in connection with "grammatical gender," a very rich and tricky question on which I shall offer a few notes in an appendix at the end of this essay.[8] Notably, German does not have a term that corresponds exactly. Without going into detail, German has "*Geschlecht*" which means "gender" and "sex" at the same time. Thus Freudian German only has the opposition "*Geschlecht/sexual.*" In fact, when they translate English texts, Germans are led—and this is important because it amounts to a veritable interpretation—to translate the English "sex" by "biological sex," and "gender" by "sociological sex," which is already, and obviously, an entire theoretical option itself—one which remains undiscussed.

Terms and concepts are weapons, weapons of war: gender against sex and, one could say, gender and sex allied against the *sexual*. Gender against sex in Stoller because under the single banner of gender he removes all conflictuality from a large part of the problematic of gender. The German author Reimut Reiche devoted an article titled "Gender ohne Sex" (1997)[9] to the way in

---

[8]   Cf. "Appendix II: Linguistic gender."
[9]   This title is a mixture of the English words "gender" and "sex" and a German word (*ohne*): "Gender without Sex."

which, in his view, the introduction of gender—"gender without sex"—leads to a biased conceptualization that completely erases the problem of sex and sexuality. Notably, Reiche criticizes the notion of "imprinting" and especially of a non-conflictual imprint, which belongs to Stoller's attempt to define gender. But it seems to me that what Reiche does not see is that the gender/sex pair serves as an even more formidable machine against the Freudian discovery.

It is here that the feminist movements as a whole enter the battle. Whether or not they are "differentialists," as it is said, in the end the sex/gender binary is always more or less preserved. In de Beauvoir, the distinction between the terms is not posed; I mean that at the time of her book the difference between the category of sex and the category of gender was not yet explicit but was, as can be shown, already functioning implicitly. One could say that her general position is that biological sex must be postulated as a foundation, even if this foundation must be completely subverted. I cite a passage from *The Second Sex*:

> Certainly these facts [of biology, of the physical differences between men and women] cannot be denied—but in themselves they have no significance… It is not merely as a body, but rather as a body subject to taboos, to laws, that the subject is conscious of himself and attains fulfilment. (de Beauvoir 1988, 66-8)

THIS IS EVIDENTLY A PASSAGE characteristic of the atmosphere—let us call it voluntarist and existentialist—in which this book was written (a book which in other respects continues to be very interesting because of its numerous descriptions). Yet it is clear that there is a double movement in the work of most feminists—the most theoretical and the most radical. There is a first movement, which subverts the notion of sex to the point of annihilating it, in a purely retroactive fashion, by gender; and then there is a moment when it is realized that, in spite of everything, it is necessary to postulate something foundational, a sort of pure nature, or, as de Beauvoir says, "facts" that "in themselves...have no significance," even if it is precisely to subvert and annihilate it.

This is the case with Judith Butler, whose second book, *Bodies that Matter* (1993), constitutes a thorough revision of her first, *Gender Trouble* (1990), in that it immediately reintroduces the "biological" aspect of "sex" and its "constraints," explaining that their omission in the preceding work had the "good tactical reason" of acting as a counterbalance: "doesn't everybody else talk about that?" (Osborne 1996, 112).

This is the case with Nicole-Claude Matthieu (1991), one of whose articles, which is extremely difficult, is titled "Three modes of conceptualization of the relation between sex and gender." You can see from the title alone that in the end she still needs the notion of sex. Gender, she says, can "translate" sex, or can "symbolize" sex or can "construct" sex, which is to say, construct it by reconstructing it, even "by destroying it." But this positions sex as a kind of biological precondition, since gender "translates," "symbolizes" or "constructs" a sex that is already there before it. Thus, implicitly or even surreptitiously, a sort of biological definition of sex is ultimately restored.

Here is a more recent passage by Nicole-Claude Matthieu: "As with the replacement of the term 'race' by the term 'ethnic group,' to leave sex out of gender risks preserving its status as an inescapable reality by forgetting that biology, and *chiefly* the physiology of fertility, is *largely* dependent on social environment" (Matthieu 2000, 197-98). I have emphasized the words "chiefly" and "largely" in this excerpt. You see that in a body of thought that aims at great rigor, she nonetheless introduces large tracts of indeterminacy by saying that biology is "chiefly" the physiology of fertility. If it is "chiefly" so, then it could nonetheless also be something else. That it is "largely" dependent on social environment means that it may not be totally dependent on it, etc. "Chiefly": sex is accepted in the domain of procreation. "Largely": one escapes by a partial dependence.[10]

In short, the feminists in general, including the "radicals"—or, one could say, the less radical of the

---

[10] Unless one goes as far as the radicalism of certain feminists who, in order to suppress the notion of sex completely, find themselves led to combat the very notion of difference at the level of logic (e.g. Monique Wittig). But I can only gesture towards this point here.

radicals—need sex in order to subvert and "denaturalize" it in gender. But is it necessary to return to the good old sex/gender sequence and in the following order: sex before gender, nature before culture, even if one agrees to "denature" nature?[11] Of course, in all of this, the Freudian *sexual* risks becoming a major absence. Psychoanalysis is mentioned but as something listed under the class of ideologies which subordinate gender to sex, the first being the "translation" of the second (Matthieu).

Does introducing gender into psychoanalysis entail allying oneself with those who would banalize the Freudian discovery? Or paradoxically would it be a way to reaffirm the *sexual* as the intimate enemy of gender?

I have at least one excuse for introducing gender into Freudian psychoanalytic thought: it has a presence, more or less sketchy, throughout Freud. To be sure, he never used the term; the German language scarcely permits him to because "*Geschlecht*" means both "sex" and "gender"; the word *Geschlecht* is used even in connection with humankind [*le genre humain*]. Thus Freud lacks the word, even though it could probably be reinvented in German

---

[11] It is precisely here that I am opposed to hastily positioning (and translating into French) *gender* as "psychosocial sex" and *sex* as "biological sex." Such a categorization reduces the gender-sex opposition to the old sociology/biology refrain, whereas the opposition is much more fruitful and complex. Further on I shall show in particular that the sex that enters into a symbolic relation with gender is not the sex of biology but in large part the sex of a fantasy anatomy, profoundly marked by the condition of the *human* animal.

using the scholarly term "*Genus*."[12] But although the word "gender" is lacking, the thing is not completely absent. Freud insists—I recall this briefly—on the existence within the human being of three pairs of opposites: "active-passive" and "phallic-castrated" but also, which is what interests us here, the third, "masculine-feminine." He tells us that the third pair is the most difficult to think; it may even be essentially resistant to thought. At the two ends of the evolution that leads to adulthood, one finds the masculinity-femininity enigma. In the adult, it is the enigma of something that is neither purely biological, nor purely psychological, nor purely sociological, but a curious mixture of the three. As Freud says: "When you meet a human being, the first distinction that you make is 'male or female?' and you are accustomed to make the distinction with unhesitating certainty" (Freud 1933, 113). The "first sight" of a human being, of a fellow creature, differentiates in an "unthought" way between masculine and feminine. At the other end, and this interests us even more, at the other end we have a famous text, "On the Sexual Theories of Children" (1908), where Freud creates the amusing and curious hypothesis of a traveller who comes from another planet (from Sirius let's say) and whose curiosity is aroused by the presence of these two "sexes." If one wished to modify Freud's text slightly one would have to say "genders," for it is actually the "habitus" of these two

---

[12] A term used in relation to linguistic "gender" but whose usage could have been enlarged.

categories of human being that counts and not the genital organs as such, which are usually concealed.

Further on I shall come back to this problem of the *enigma* because in this case the human being is not envisaged in terms of a succession, whereby the child becomes adult or whereby the adult recalls the child that he was, but rather in terms of a simultaneity: it is the child *in the presence of* the adult who asks himself the question about this difference present in adults. But Freud very often forgets this questioning. What I mean is that the category of gender is often absent or unthought. One could mention, for example, the whole problematic that Freud constructs concerning homosexuality and paranoia in the Schreber case. Freud writes the basic statement, which he will play with by modifying each of its terms, in the following way: "*I* (a man) *love him* (a man)" (1911, 63). Furthermore, we know how Freud's entire dialectic concerning the different modes of delusion consists of modifying the "I" of "I love," the "him" of "him (a man)" and also, of course, the verb "to love" which can be transformed into "to hate." Thus, the whole dialectic of "I (a man) / I love him (a man)" is centred on the *second part of the sentence* without ever calling into question what is meant by "I, a man." To do so would constitute a problematic, however, that is precisely that of Schreber himself, and which with good reason many analysts have aligned with that of transsexualism.

In psychoanalysis, and generally in clinical practice,

the vast majority of "observations"—if not all of them—begin unthinkingly with: "This is a 30-year-old man…" or "A woman of 25…" Is gender truly non-conflictual to the point of being unquestioningly assumed from the beginning? Has gender, so to speak, expelled the conflictual outside of itself in the form of the *sexual*?

*

*   *

I NOW COME TO MY second part, which is the history of the gender-sex-*sexual* triad. By "history" I mean purely and simply the infantile genesis of this triad in the human being, the little human being; a genesis that psychoanalysts must not hesitate to approach.

There generally exists a kind of foundational "adulto-centrism." I have spoken of the feminists but they are certainly not the only ones—one could say the same thing of the ethnologists. I say this about ethnologists because, if you take Lévi-Strauss, for example, the theory of the incest prohibition is a theory situated entirely on the level of the adult. Besides, the major incest prohibition in Lévi-Strauss is the prohibition against sororal incest, which clearly shows that it is a question of adults of the same age, a world of only adults. There certainly is a post-Cartesian prejudice there, a kind of adulto-centrism that is not even close to being abolished.

In a few lines that were circulated before this

presentation, I have contrasted two sentences: de Beauvoir's, "One is not born a woman, but becomes one" (1988, 295) and Freud's, "In conformity with its peculiar nature, psycho-analysis does not try to describe what a woman is—that would be a task it could scarcely perform—but sets about enquiring how she comes into being" (1933, 116).

One could say many things about the similarities between these two sentences. First of all and strikingly, de Beauvoir in 1949 does not feel the need to cite Freud's statement, which is so close to her own. Although quite close, it is certainly different; and yet, in spite of everything, it is the precursor to her work.

In what respect are they close and in what respect remote? They are remote insofar as, in a certain way, one could say that de Beauvoir shows herself more "naturalist" than Freud. She accepts "woman" as a being, as a given, as a sort of nature, a raw given that evidently one is led to take up subjectively, whether to become it or to refuse it. "She becomes *it*." In Freud, on the other hand, we have something quite extraordinary in that his statement is completely contradictory. Freud tells us: "She becomes what we are incapable of *defining*." In a certain sense, Freud is here more existentialist than Simone de Beauvoir. One could also situate them in *the dispute over "afterwardsness."* On one side, that of de Beauvoir, we have retroactive interpretation, the omnipotence of changing afterwards the meaning of the past, "resignification": this was already the Jungian thesis of *Zurückphantasieren*, "retrospective fantasizing." In this line of thought there is the "performative," gender as performative, as certain feminists say. On the other side, that of Freud, there is determinism, which is also confirmed at the end of the lecture on femininity in *New Introductory Lectures*, where Freud accentuates this determinism in a caricatured and rather unpleasant way, in order to assert that a woman, once she has become an adult, has a "psychic rigidity" and "unchangeability" that he has never encountered in young men of the same age (1933, 134-5). The responsibility for this assertion I leave entirely to him.

Thus one could identify a point of view that splits de Beauvoir-Freud on the question of afterwardsness between "retroactive modification"—the action of the future and of the present upon the past—and "deferred action"—a determinism, however delayed it may be, of the present by the past. I have tried to go beyond this split by introducing two essential elements into afterwardsness: one element is the *primacy of the other* which, because they remain in the frame *of a single* individual, is precisely what these conceptions of afterwardsness do not mention. They do not bring the presence of the other into play in the process of afterwardsness. The second element, equally lacking from these conceptions, is child-adult *simultaneity*. What I mean is that the child-adult couple should not be conceived essentially in terms of one succeeding the other, but rather of one actually finding itself in the presence of the other—concretely so, in the first years of life, from the first months. I think that *the key to the notion of afterwardsness* is to take it beyond the consideration of just the single individual, where one remains enclosed in an opposition with no exit: asking whether the child is the cause of the adult, or whether the adult freely reinterprets the child; asking whether determinism follows the arrow of time or whether, on the contrary, it moves in the opposite direction. It is an opposition that can only be overcome if one positions the individual in the presence of the other, if one positions the child *in the presence* of the adult and as *receiving messages* from the adult, messages that are not a *raw given,* but are "to be translated" (cf. Fletcher 1999, 260-5).

So, for this talk I have proposed, *in this order*, "gender, sex, the *sexual*." To speak of the little human being in this order is to put gender in first place. *It is therefore to call into question the primacy of sexual difference as a foundation.*

Subjectively speaking—and here the discussions and the observations are quite numerous—nothing permits the claim that biological sex is intimately perceived, apprehended and lived by the subject in any way at all in the first months of life. Here I have in mind texts such as that of Person and Ovesey (1983), which Kernberg summarizes in his book on "love relations" (1995), and in particular Roiphe and Galenson's book on *The Infantile Origins of Sexual Identity* (1981), which was published in French some years ago.

Gender, according to all these authors and according to all the observations they report—I cannot cite them here but they are completely convincing—gender would be first in time and in becoming conscious, and it would start to become stable toward the end of the first year. But—and we must immediately add a *but*—gender is *neither* a hypothetical cerebral impregnation, which would be a sort of hormonal impregnation (although we know that there is a certain perinatal hormonal impregnation; it ends rapidly and has *no* influence on the choice of gender), *nor* an imprint in Stoller's sense, *nor* a habit. All these notions are, in the end, what I call "ipso-centrist," which is to say centred on the individual alone.

To define gender in my sense, and I am not alone in saying this, the crucial term is "*assignment*." Assignment underlines the primacy of the other in the process—whether the first assignment is the declaration at the town hall, at the church or in some other official place, a declaration involving the assignment of a first name, the assignment to a place in a kinship network, etc., or very often the assignment to membership in a religion. But I want to emphasize this important point: it is a process that is not discrete, not done once and for all, not limited to a single act. In this I distinguish myself clearly from all that could be said, for example, of "determination by the name." This is a field already opened up by Stekel, but which only received further development (partly unwarranted) with the Lacanian inflation of the notion of the signifier. That the assignment of the first name can carry unconscious messages is one thing. But the "signifier" is not a determining factor in itself. Assignment is a complex ensemble of acts that go on within language and within the meaningful behaviour of the family circle. One could speak of an ongoing assignment, of a veritable *prescription*. Prescription in the sense in which one speaks of messages called "prescriptives"; it is therefore of the order of the message, even a bombardment of messages.

A word of warning! It is said that "gender is social," "sex is biological." Caution must be taken with the term "social," because here it covers up at least two realities that intersect. On the one hand there is the social, or the socio-cultural, in general. Of course it is in "the social" that the assignment is inscribed, if only in that famous declaration at the beginning of life that is made at the level of the institutional structures of a given society. But the inscriber is not the social in general; it is the little group of close *socii*, of friends and blood relations. This is, effectively, the father, the mother, a friend, a brother, a cousin, etc. Thus it is the little group of *socii* who inscribe *in* the social, but it is not Society that does the assigning.[13]

This idea of assignment or of "identification by"

GENDER, SEX, AND THE *SEXUAL*

---

[13] At the beginning of *Group Psychology and the Analysis of the Ego* (1921) Freud affirms that "...from the very first, individual psychology... is at the same time social psychology as well" (69). But one quickly sees that the "social psychology" of which he speaks is that of close interactions within the narrow circle of the *socius*: "his parents and...his brothers and sisters,...the object of his love, and...his physician" (70).

completely changes the vector of identification. Here there is a way to get out of the aporia of Freud's "O so beautiful" formula which has caused so much thought and commentary: "an individual's first and most important identification, his identification with the father in his own personal prehistory" (1923, 31). As you know, this beautiful formula is immediately contradicted by a note in which Freud says: "Perhaps it would be safer to say 'with the parents'; for before a child has arrived at definite knowledge of the difference between the sexes, the lack of a penis, it does not distinguish in value between its father and its mother" (1923, 31n1).[14] This primitive identification with the father of personal prehistory, which has been revived as "symbolic" identification by certain Lacanians (I am thinking of Florence [1978], for example, in his work on identification), is considered more or less the matrix of the ego ideal. I simply ask the following question, or rather I propose this: instead of being an "identification with," wouldn't this be an *"identification by"?* In other words, I would say: "primitive identification *by* the socius of personal prehistory."

Because I am not the first to go in this direction, I shall pause for breath a moment to cite Person and Ovesey in their very important article on the question of gender identity. Person and Ovesey completely invert the commonly accepted sequence—that is, of the biological

---

14   For a critique of these passages of Freud's, which are absolutely enigmatic and symptomatic, cf. Laplanche 1980, 335-7.

coming before the social—by saying the following (you will see which aspects can be accepted and which can be criticized or modified): "In this sense, one can say that gender precedes sexuality in development and organizes sexuality, not the reverse" (Person 1999, 70). A formula that I accept, though only partially. As to the idea of precedence, you can see that I subscribe to this absolutely—that is to say, to the precedence of gender in relation to anything else. As to the term "sexuality," I think it is too vague to be accepted (except as a sort of general term, a kind of bridging term). For my part, I would say, "gender precedes sex"; and furthermore, differing from Person and Ovesey, who say, "gender precedes sex and organizes it," I would say, "Yes, gender precedes sex. But, far from organizing it, it is organized by it."

I am tempted here to call upon the schema of what I have called the "general theory of seduction." The general theory of seduction starts from the idea of messages from the other. In these messages, there is a code or a carrier wave, that is to say a basic language, which is a conscious/preconscious language. In other words, I have never said—I do not think I have ever said—that there are unconscious messages from the parents. On the contrary, I think that there are conscious/preconscious messages and that the parental unconscious is like the "noise"—in the sense of communication theory—that comes to perturb and *to compromise* the conscious/preconscious message.

But the code, or the language that corresponds to a

code—the carrier language—is not necessarily always the same. Until now, in the general theory of seduction, which aims to explain the genesis of the drive, I have mainly focused on the code of *attachment* in so far as it is carried by bodily care given to the child. Thus, in this case, communication takes place within the attachment relation. Here, today, I try to advance a second, more hypothetical step that demands to be articulated with the former. Communication does not only occur with the language of bodily care; there is also the social code, the social language; there are also the messages of the *socius*: these messages are chiefly *messages of gender assignment*. But they are also the carriers of a good deal of "noise," all that is brought by the adults who are close to the child: parents, grand-parents, brothers and sisters, their fantasies, their unconscious or preconscious expectations. A father may consciously assign the masculine gender to his offspring but have expected a daughter, even have unconsciously desired to penetrate a daughter. Actually, this field of the unconscious relation of parents to their children has been very poorly explored; the first messages are generally maternal (but not necessarily solely maternal), and I don't think that the parental unconscious is limited to infiltrating the care given to the infant's body. These unconscious wishes also infiltrate the assignment of gender. Therefore it's what is "sexed" and also and above all the "*sexual*" of the parents that *makes a noise* in the assignment. I say the *sexual* above all because I want to hold onto the idea that adults in the presence of a child will, most importantly, reactivate their own *infantile sexuality*.

The theory of seduction, as I have attempted to formulate it, postulates a translation, and so a translation code. Here it is evidently on the side of sex that one must search. Gender is acquired, assigned, but enigmatic, until about fifteen months. Sex comes to stabilize and to translate gender in the course of the second year, in what Roiphe and Galenson call "the early genital phase."

The *castration complex* is at the centre of it. Of course it offers some certainties, but these very certainties are too clear-cut and must be questioned. The certainty of the castration complex is based upon ideology and illusion. Freud said: "Destiny is anatomy."[15] This destiny is that there are two sexes, separated, he says, by "The Anatomical Distinction Between the Sexes" (1925, 243). But here Freud's argument cannot dispense with a certain sleight of hand, which consists in introducing a confusion between *anatomy* and *biology*. Indeed, at other moments, he speaks of the "bedrock" of biology, in effect making this destiny a biological fate. Many people see an affirmation of Freud's "biologism" in the phrase "Anatomy is destiny." But *anatomy* is not biology, nor is it physiology, and still less is it hormonal determinism. There are several levels (not to mention other registers) within anatomy itself: there

GENDER, SEX, AND THE SEXUAL

123

---

[15] As a translation, this is preferable to "Anatomy is destiny." German permits the phrase to be translated in this way, and I believe it is more striking to say "Destiny is anatomy."

is scientific anatomy, which may be purely descriptive or may be structural—for example, the anatomy of specific apparatuses, which describes the function of the genital apparatus on the basis of its anatomical structure—and then there is "popular" anatomy. But the anatomy that is a "destiny" is a "popular" anatomy, and moreover it is perceptual, even purely illusory. "Perceptual" in what respect? In animals that do not have an upright posture there are *two* groups of external genitals *perceived* as such, that is to say visualized as such, the female genital organs being perfectly perceptible—visible and also, above all, perceived by smell. So, for the animal there are *two sexes*. For man, owing to his erect posture, there is a double perceptual loss: the loss or regression of olfactory perception, and the loss of the sight of the external female genital organs. Perception is then reduced to what Freud sometimes calls "inspection" (*Inspektion*), that is to say pure visualization in the medical sense of the term. For the human being, the perception of genital organs is no longer the perception of *two* genital organs but of only one. The difference between the sexes becomes a "difference of sex."

In Spinoza there is a passage of which I'm especially fond, which does not seem to do anything but in reality works perfectly. He says: "For the intellect and will that would constitute the essence of God would have to be vastly different from human intellect and will, and would have no point of agreement except the name. They could be no more alike than the celestial constellation of the dog and the dog that barks" (Spinoza 2006, 15). Well, this is a disparity between two things that actually have nothing in common except the name: "the celestial constellation of the dog" and "the dog that barks." I would say that this can be transposed onto the question of the difference of the sexes: the perceptible difference of sex as sign or as signifier has practically nothing to do with biological and physiological male/female difference.

Isn't *this contingency an extraordinary destiny?* The erect posture makes the female organs perceptually inaccessible; but this contingency has been raised by many civilizations, and no doubt our own, to the rank of a major, universal, signifier of presence/absence.

Is perceptual anatomical difference a language, a code? It is certainly not a complete code, but it is at the least something that structures a code—a most rigid code at that, structured precisely by the law of the excluded third, by presence/absence. It is rather a skeleton of a code, but of a logical code that for a long time I have referred to as "phallic logic" (Laplanche 1980). This is the logic of presence/absence, of zero and one, which has received an impressive expansion in the modern universe of computer science.

Thus it is difficult to disengage the question of the difference of sex from the castration complex.

Once disentangled from certain ideological presuppositions, studies such as those by Roiphe and Galenson, long-term observations of an entire population of closely observed children, appear emphatically to reinforce the idea of a very widespread, even universal castration complex. But in contrast to Freud, the castration complex according to Roiphe and Galenson is not initially bound up with the Oedipus. They speak of an "early genital phase," a "castration reaction," which is actually a reaction *by* means of the castration complex.

Many questions may be opened up here—those that I evoked quite a while back in one of my *Problématiques* called *Castration, Symbolisation* where I asked whether the universality of the castration complex in its rigid form, with its logical opposition of "phallic/castrated," is inevitable, or whether there are more flexible, more varied, more ambivalent models of symbolization.

Does the inevitability of the logic of the excluded third in the equipment of our western civilization necessarily go hand in hand with the reign of the castration complex at the level of the individual or of the little group, which is to say as *ideology*? After all, in analyses, memories bound to the castration complex are often encountered in attenuated form: attenuated in that they are compromised by what they seek to repress.

Yet what they seek to repress is precisely "the *sexual*." What sex and, as one might say, its secular arm, the castration complex, tend to repress is infantile sexuality. Repress it or, more precisely, create it by repressing it.

Here I can only mention what recently emerged from a dialogue with Daniel Widlöcher concerning "attachment and infantile sexuality" (see Laplanche 2011, 27-51). Infantile sexuality, the "*sexual*," is the very object of psychoanalysis. It is drive-based, and not instinctual. It functions according to a particular economic regime that seeks tension rather than the reduction of tension, and it has the fantasy object at its source and not at its end-point, thus reversing the "object relation." Consequently the *sexual* will occupy the entire domain and attempt to organize itself but in a way that is always precarious, until the upheaval of puberty when the genital instincts will have to come to terms with it.

I shall shortly close this presentation in order to give way to discussion, which is to say to uncertainties.

*
* *

I WANTED TO PROVIDE A precise framework in order to open up some hypotheses and some uncertainties. As to the *hypotheses*, some of these profoundly unsettle commonly accepted views:

— Precedence of gender: gender comes before sex, a point that upends habits of thought, the ruts of routine thought that put the "biological" before the "social."

— Precedence of assignment: assignment comes before symbolization.

— Primary identification: far from being a primary identification "with" (the adult), this is, I propose, a primary identification "by" (the adult).

— The contingent, perceptual and illusory character of anatomical sexual difference, the veritable destiny of modern civilization.

As to the *UNCERTAINTIES*: these are numerous, and I'm sure you will raise them. I shall point to the question of knowing how the two lines of enigmatic messages which I am currently trying to define come to be combined: that is to say, we must make room for the second line, that of social assignment, next to the line of attachment. How are the problems of femininity and bisexuality to be positioned with respect to this double line? What is the relation between what I have suggested concerning "identification by" and the notion of the ego ideal? I have certainly not addressed all of the uncertainties, the questions and the objections that you will want to raise.

APPENDIX I

STOLLER AND GENDER

I WOULD LIKE TO START off by *noting a few impressions* that arise from reading Stoller—Stoller as researcher and thinker.[1]

Stoller shows a strikingly impressive freedom of style, in fact he flaunts it. He doesn't hesitate to criticize and reconsider his own observations (e.g., in Chapter 5 of *Presentations of Gender* [1985], "How Biology Can Contribute to Gender Identity"). Sometimes he makes fun of himself, or of explanations that are too complete. Among many other examples, there is the moment in *Perversion* (1975, 81–82) where he throws into a single rag-bag non-analytic psychological or physiological theories as well as analytic theories, and concludes that "psychoanalytic theory is the most syncretic system since the Pantheon of the Romans" (1975, 82n).

Or again (1985, 3–4) he criticizes psychoanalytic jargon, while also showing a mistrust of "case reports" (2 and 9)—a mistrust concerning theory that can, however, end up in a curious scepticism: "A last hopeless mutter: of what practical importance is it whether perversions are classified as neuroses or as something different?" (1975,

---

[1] Works referred to: *Sex and Gender* (1984 [orig. 1968]); *Perversion: the Erotic Form of Hatred* (1986 [orig. 1975]); *Presentations of Gender* (1985).

101n).

Excessively simplistic biological explanations are shown no mercy, especially those drawn from animal experimentation concerning the erection centre in monkeys (1975, 21–22); Stoller returns here to explanations that take account of fantasy, while underlining the fact that fantasy is no less neurophysiological than the rest. Similarly, in Chapter 5 of *Presentations of Gender* (1985) cited above, he finally gives pre-eminence to the individual acquisition of gender over the hypothesis of hormonal determinism.

Nevertheless, Stoller's positions in relation to biology remain ambiguous. One has the impression that he sprinkles his writings with allusions to sexual physiology so as to avoid dealing with the question in real depth. One of the most explicit passages is in *Perversion* (1975, 15ff), but in the end the confusion is only multiplied. Here Stoller starts out from a passage in which Freud speaks of the biological "bedrock" (1937, 252) without noticing that Freud himself performs a sleight of hand by equating the anatomical difference of the *observable external genital organs* with a biological difference.

Stoller goes on to refer to the Freudian notion of complementary series, which positions the "constitutional" (innate, endogenous, atavistic) in opposition to the "accidental" (acquired, exogenous).

However, by an unjustified slippage this opposition is superimposed onto the opposition between the biological and the psychosocial.

innate	acquired
biological	psychological-social

This assimilation is unwarranted and misleading: it encourages a return to the old soul-body problematic and it neglects:

1. the fact that the biological can have a mental expression (hunger) and that the mental necessarily has a neurophysiological counterpart;

2. the fact that there may be biological characteristics that are acquired, even at the level of the individual, and that there is a given, pre-existing "psychosocial" domain (social categories, symbolic systems, etc.).

THE CRITICISM OF SIMPLISTIC THINKING or of the useless complication of current explanations falls flat when confronted with the extremely simplistic aspects of certain Stollerian developments. For example, the summaries that Stoller gives of Freudian theory are so cursory and superficial that one wonders where or even whether he has really read Freud at all.

For example, in chapter 8 of *Perversion*, we read among other things that "[Freud] saw homosexuality in males especially as a pathology of the resolution of a boy's oedipal conflict with his father" (1975, 144). A purported summary that is completely silent about the maternal aetiology (cf. the Leonardo text), which, in addition, Stoller attributes to other authors: "others emphasized that male homosexuality, which seemed to Freud to spring primarily from a son's disturbed relationship with his father, could be traced back to preoedipal disturbances in mother-son relationships" (ibid.). Furthermore Stoller attributes this to some of the "moderns," without mentioning the "Leonardo theory" that can be found regularly in Freud.

Stoller's capacity for mockery and his freedom of style can be seductive, but they all too often mark an absence of serious thinking. This applies not only to his reading of Freud, but to his own thought. Take his explanation of "perversion." The suggestive title *Perversion: the Erotic Form of Hatred* (1975) does not live up to its promise. For the "hatred" in question has nothing to do with the death drive or with unbinding; in the end it is related, in an unambiguous fashion and apropos of all perversions, to a desire for vengeance experienced by the boy, following a humiliation ("trauma") undergone in childhood.

Another type of explanation, reduced to a strict minimum, is that which relates transsexualism to "too much mother, too little father" (1985, 28, 63), a formula so general and so abstract that one can find it in innumerable attempts to identify a psychogenesis of neuroses, psychoses and perversions, all the way up to and including Lacanian foreclosure (although Lacan had criticized this type of "lame reply" in advance) (Lacan 1959, 480).

On the same level of theoretical prestidigitation, one

will note the answer to the question: how is femininity transmitted? Stoller says: "I do not know…I doubt if there is a more intense way available to humans for merging with each other than to look deeply into each other's eyes; lovers have always known this, as have mothers…Perhaps in this way, especially, the boys drink in, merge with, sense they are a part of their mothers' femaleness" (Stoller 1985, 33).

Another subterfuge, mostly used when criticisms of his theory accumulate, consists in acknowledging that what he is describing (the "primary transsexual," the "very feminine" boy) is an extremely rare condition that may never have existed (ibid., 40–42) or is only an identikit picture.

*

*   *

LET US ENTER INTO THE *question of gender*, without losing sight of what serves as a point of reference for Stoller: the discourse of adult transsexuals, and, to a certain degree, the discourse and/or behaviour of "very feminine" boys.

The central affirmation of this discourse is: "I have the soul of a woman in the body of a man." Taken at face value, it is a discourse that confirms *gender* as something psychological, as a matter of belief, and which affirms *sex* as a purely somatic reality. Gender would be the subjective aspect, the consciousness of sex. Although Stoller sometimes maintains the soul-body dichotomy, he only partially adheres to it.

A more tautological but perhaps more interesting definition is found in *Presentations of Gender* (1985, 10–11). Here, gender is defined as the belief or feeling that one belongs to one of the two genders. Thus, the transsexual does not believe that he is of the female sex, but of the female *gender*. One sees that we are pulled toward several convergent ideas: "a dense mass of beliefs" and "convictions"; the feeling of belonging to a group (one of the two large human groups); and, finally, an element that is situated on the side of the subject or the ego, and not on the side of the object or "object choice."

My commentary on this—not Stoller's—would be as follows: gender choice, even if it is correlated with object choice, is fundamentally different from it. Recall Freud's basic formula in the Schreber case: "I (a man) love him (a man)" (1911, 63). In this formula the "I" may be (or may consider himself to be) a man or a woman: this is the question of gender. So again in the formula for homosexuality in the Leonardo case study, Freud establishes the following connection:

Mother – loves – Leonardo
Leonardo – loves – a boy in the image of the child Leonardo.

For all that, Leonardo is not identified with the gender

of the mother whose place he takes. The genesis of *gender* is thus clearly independent of the genesis of object choice.

Let us now turn to the aetiology that Stoller postulates as the origin of gender identity. In *Presentations of Gender* (1985, 11–12), Stoller sums up this aetiology according to five factors:

1. A biologic force

2. Sex assignment at birth

3. The attitudes of the parents (the way in which the child is perceived and raised)

4. "Biopsychic phenomena"

5. The developing body ego

SOME OF THESE FACTORS ARE eliminated or regrouped:

No. 5, the developing body ego, corresponds to different self-perceptions by the child of its own sexed body (ibid., 14). But Stoller eliminates this last factor as being secondary in the little child: "Even when anatomy is defective…the individual develops an unequivocal sense of maleness or femaleness if the sex assignment and rearing are unequivocal" (ibid.). Stoller often combines factors 2 and 3 (assignment + parental attitudes). This leaves three factors to be discussed.

A. *The biologic force*

The influence of genetic and hormonal factors on gender choice is fiercely debated; indeed there are two ways to conceptualise this influence. The idea of hormonal determination in the "brain" (a somewhat debatable idea, from an experimental point of view) may, theoretically speaking, be manifested:

— directly by a male or female "psyche," though there is nothing to bear this out (cf. the two notes on Stoller 1985, 22 and 23);

— or indirectly through the determination by the "brain" of anatomical appearance. This then returns the matter to our factor of "assignment + parental attitudes." This second option is clearly preferred by Stoller. I can only make reference to the long case report and the related follow-up data presented in chapter 5: "How Biology can Contribute to Gender Identity."

Thus the only factors left in play are "biopsychic phenomena" and "assignment + parental attitudes." Since Stoller's own theory remains essentially that of "biopsychic phenomena," I shall begin with that factor.

B. Under the term "biopsychic phenomena"

The notion of biopsychic phenomena comprises an entire theory founded on the idea of *symbiosis*, which turns up repeatedly. It can be found on p.16ff. and p.25ff. (in chapter 3, "An Emphasis on Mothers"); and also, for example, in *Perversion* (1985) chapter 8 ("Symbiosis Anxiety and the Development of Masculinity").

The essential reference point is the theory of Margaret Mahler, and it is difficult for us in France to imagine the hold this notion has had on Anglo-Saxon thought from 1952 almost until the present day.

In a word, Margaret Mahler inferred from the observation of *autistic* and *symbiotic* children the postulate that in the course of its development every child necessarily passed through these two phases, to which the subject could subsequently regress. On the other hand, a normal development is presumed to entail a "separation-individuation" phase in terms of the child's relation to the mother, an evolution that Mahler was led to divide into four sub-phases.

To be sure, this theory had some influence in France. But very quickly it was sharply criticized, both in its own right and by virtue of its affinity with the Freudian theory of a primary narcissism understood in the literal sense, that is, as something that exists from the first days of life. Here I can only mention in outline a few stages of this critiqu.[2]

For a critique that is much more recent and is based on

---

[2] See Laplanche and Pontalis (1973); and refer to the index at the end of *Nouveaux fondements pour la psychanalyse* (Laplanche 2008, 187). See also the arguments against Winnicott's idea of a "first not-me possession," which presupposes an original lack of differentiation between mother and child (*Nouveaux fondements* index, ibid., 172). See Jean Gortais (1987).

child observation, one should refer to Martin Dornes and to the cluster of arguments he assembles (Dornes 2002).

Dornes's article demolishes the idea of a primitive symbiotic phase in the child, acknowledging that at most there are symbiotic *moments* in *some* children.

The way in which Stoller adheres to Mahlerism is, however, quite peculiar:

1. He doesn't care at all about the "autistic phase."

2. He postulates that in the process of going from symbiosis to separation-individuation there is a particular symbiosis, one that is gendered and is *different from symbiosis in general.* In other words, in the case of "primary transsexuals" the boy could *separate himself from the mother* and become completely independent of her in all other respects, but *without managing to separate himself from the femininity of his mother* (Stoller 1985, 16–18).

As to the aetiology, we have seen that it always comes back to "too much mother, not enough father," a generalization in which Stoller, good "scientist" that he is, would like to find elements of predictability (if a mother is like that, the son will be like this. If a son is like this, the mother must have been like that [1985, 33–34]). However, this desired predictability is at odds with the fact that one practically never finds the exemplary case of a son who is "like this," that is to say a pure "primary transsexual."

Stoller affirms that:

1. cases of "very feminine boys" are a small minority and should not be confused with homosexuals (41);

2. he has never followed one of these "very feminine boys" so far into adulthood as to be able to see them transform into 'primary transexuals';

3. not one of the cases followed by Richard Green became a "primary transsexual" (41n12).

When Stoller tries, in one case, to demonstrate "predictability" (38ff.), it concerns a boy who did not begin to dress as a girl until 3 ¾ years old and whose description is profoundly at odds with the "type" (or identikit picture) described previously (19ff.).

Conclusion

THE STOLLERIAN EXPLANATION OF GENDER identity collapses on all sides:

1. Its Mahlerian foundation is contested. Already in the debate with Stern in *Presentations of Gender* (Stoller 1985, 39n9, 39–40) one can see all the "complementary hypotheses" that Stoller is forced to demand his reader accept in order to try to "save" a theory that is contradicted by the facts. At that

point, when the Mahlerian foundation collapses (a debate that I shall not take up again here), the whole Stollerian aetiology collapses.

2. In addition, the latent idea according to which symbiosis = identification is thoroughly questionable. The biological model of symbiosis implies complementarity and not assimilation. Why would it be otherwise in a "psychic" "symbiosis"?

3. Even supposing that there is a primary identification with the *mother* (whether or not by means of symbiosis), why would this be a primary identification with the mother as a *woman*? And why in particular with *femininity*, which is a very elaborated trait?

4. Why would "disidentification" (Greenson's term) or "separation-individuation" (Mahler's terms), succeed on all levels *except* on the level of gender? How could such a split be conceived? (cf. 40–41).

5. The appearance of masculine and feminine traits happens when the child begins to be socialised (at the end of the first year and the beginning of the second). Who would say of a nursling that it is a masculine rather than a feminine creature (even if *we* project: "It's a boy!")?

Nevertheless, Stoller's work has the following immense merits:

1. To have underlined the early appearance of gender identity.

2. To have, in his moments of greatest lucidity (1985, 73ff.), attributed gender identity to the complex unity created by "assignment" and the "endless messages reflecting parents' attitudes delivered to the child's body and psyche" (ibid., 74–75) (one can see a door opening up to the general theory of seduction). Finally, of the three factors singled out above the only one remaining is "assignment + parental attitudes" (factors 2 and 3 of his aetiological series).

In the very important ending of Chapter 5 (ibid., 73–76), Stoller vigorously refutes the notion of the *direct hormonal determination of gender*: hormones, even when administered in massive doses, generally only lead to small or modest changes in gender behaviour. Even though, with the sceptical style he often adopts, Stoller ends on a *non liquet*, his preference is for the psychological and relational hypothesis (ibid., 75–76).

APPENDIX II

LINGUISTIC GENDER

IN WHAT FOLLOWS, WE SHALL designate as gender (S) the gender that is at stake for analysts, psychologists and social science specialists more generally. Here (S) stands for "sexological." We introduce this clarification so that in all cases in which confusion would be possible we are able to distinguish between "gender (S)" and linguistic gender, or "gender (L)." We are well aware that by introducing this (S) we are to some extent raising questions about the distinctions between gender, sex and the *sexual*.[1] But we have never claimed to be creating a categorization that would be clear-cut, as if by a knife, so to speak. Far from it! To repeat our point about assignment, gender is intrinsically freighted with contents that are conceptually "impure"; that is to say, to a great extent unconscious and bearing on sex and sexuality.

1. – We are led, then, to an important excursus on linguistics. Why venture into what might appear to be a digression?

---

[1] [*UIT Editor*: On Laplanche's French neologism "sexual" (as distinct from the normal "sexuel"), see the Editor's second footnote at the beginning of this chapter. The term is printed here in italics to mark it off from the standard English term with the same spelling.]

a. In part, the feminist (and antifeminist) battle crystallizes around gender (L). Beyond those aspects of this which are anecdotal and somewhat ridiculous—in particular, the desire to modify mental attitudes by artificially modifying language[2]—it is worth taking seriously the notion of "symbolic systems" that impose their supremacy—Bourdieu's notion of "masculine domination" being a case in point.

b. Gender (L) eminently relates to language or, more precisely, to *language as a system* [*la langue*]. Since we have a tendency to see in the assignment of gender (S) an act of *utterance* [*parole*] (a message), and to see the assumption of gender as a process that could be understood as the translation of a message, it is even more urgent to pose the *distinction* between these two types of gender (S and L), whose resemblance risks leading us down the wrong path.

2. – Throughout the course of its innumerable variations and complex historical evolutions (which

---

[2] In a separate domain, Roy Schafer's attempt to create a "new language for psychoanalysis" moved in the same direction: from the moment analyst and analysand agree to replace the substantive or the adjective "unconscious" with the adverb "unconsciously," we are already a long way on the road towards disalienation. See Oppenheimer (1984, 467).

we couldn't possibly claim to cover exhaustively), gender (L) seems to us to have entailed a tendency towards a logic of the excluded third, which irresistibly evokes the binary and exclusive logic of the castration complex (phallic—castrated; or: phallic—all the rest). To this extent, what we see emerging is that the problematic of gender (L), far from being situated at the same level as gender (S), in fact corresponds to, or at least has a tendency towards correspondence with what I call "sex," that which translates and organises gender (S).

3. – The two authors from whom we shall take our bearings (even though it means expanding our documentation) are Greville Corbett (1991) and Raoul de la Grasserie (1898).

NO DOUBT THE DIFFERENCE OF nearly one hundred years which separates these two authors gives Corbett superiority in terms of information, linguistic "scientificity," etc. Yet one cannot help but be struck by the narrowly technical and restricted character of Corbett's approach, despite the extent of his documentation.

This approach is characterized from the start by a restriction of the problematic of genders, which (following Charles F. Hockett) are narrowly defined as "classes of nouns reflected in the behaviour of associated words" (quoted in Corbett 1991, 1). Gender is a *property of the substantive* that has *consequences* for agreement (the agreement of articles, adjectives, pronouns, even of verbs, and so on).

This deliberate, technical restriction of gender mutilates the anthropological dimension of Corbett's book:

a. – Unlike La Grasserie, Corbett prohibits himself from connecting "gender" in this narrow sense with the presence of noun classes in *languages that do not require agreement* (non-inflected languages). In such languages, gender—understood in the broad sense given by La Grasserie: "families of things" (La Grasserie 1898, 624)—manifests itself in, for example, the presence of classificatory words and affixes.

Thus, in Chinese, all the names of trees are followed by the generic name: tree (*chou*) (ibid., 598).[3]

A pine would be a pine-tree (*song chou*); a pear, a pear-tree (*ly chou*). Sometimes the affix retains its meaning even when it is separate (*chou* by itself means "tree"); sometimes it has no more than a classificatory value, which is dependent on its affixed position (e.g. in Algonquin where "every second word becomes an empty word which

---

[3]   It will be immediately noticed that the notion of class or of gender in linguistics in no way implies distinction by sex. As Christophe Dejours has pointed out (1986), the number of genders (L) can vary from 2 to 20 or more, among which sexual distinction is possible but not always present. In our example, "tree" is a gender, in the same way that "insect" could be a gender, or "non-meat food," etc.

serves to form the substantive" (ibid., 600)). This is a little similar to the *e* ending in French, which is used to mark the feminine: the *e* by itself has no meaning.

This entire domain is excluded from Corbett's investigation.

> b. – Corbett asks artificially complex questions concerning what he calls "the assignment of gender," which is to say "the way in which native speakers allocate nouns to genders…How native speakers know that the word for 'house' is masculine in Russian, feminine in French and neuter in Tamil" (Corbett 1991, 3).[4]

All of which is fine so long as the subject has semantic criteria at his disposal. Thus "'house' in Tamil is neuter because it does not denote a human" (ibid.).

But the problem becomes more complicated when there are no semantic criteria: why is "house" masculine in Russian?

Corbett has, then, to make do with "phonological and morphological" criteria.

His reasoning is as follows. It would be too complicated for each speaking subject to *learn* the gender of each noun when gender is not determined by meaning. There must therefore exist formal rules (phonological or morphological) which are more or less hidden and which have not been

---

[4] Here I am summarizing, on the basis of Dejours' work.

formulated by linguists. In this regard Corbett relies on certain regularities (e.g. in French the words ending in "son" are feminine) and on experimental studies in which one presents to native speakers words borrowed from a foreign language, or words created artificially, in order to see how they make gender assignments.

Here one can see that the term "assignment" has taken on two meanings: from spontaneous assignment by a speaker, it becomes assignment by a linguist or by a subject in an experiment. Of course certain regularities are uncovered but they are not sufficient to explain how a native speaker almost never makes a mistake (see ibid., 7). Hence Corbett's quasi-mystical appeal to "hidden rules."

It seems to me that that Corbett makes a simple error with respect to both the speaking subject and the subject learning a language. It consists in making gender an intrinsic property of the noun, which is "reflected in the behaviour of associated words." This is clearly true in the context of an *experiment*, where one presents a subject with an isolated substantive: *verre* (glass). But when one learns a language (whether as a child or as an adult) one is never presented with "*verre*," but always with "*le verre*." The associated word, the article, is a part of one and the same syntagm, which the subject learns at a single stroke (it's as easy to learn "*le verre*" as to learn "*verre*"). One could even say that in French the article plays precisely the role of "gender classifier" as it is defined above on the basis of La Grasserie:

"*Le-verre*" relates "*verre*" to the masculine gender

just as

"pine-tree" relates "pine" to the gender[5] tree

4. – One more word on the term *assignment* as it is used both by linguists in relation to gender (L) and by psychologists in relation to gender (S).

Gender (L) defines noun classes.

Gender (S) applies to *classes of living or human beings*, classes which have a certain relation (yet to be determined) to sexual reproduction.

The assignment of gender (L) is a *phenomenon of language* which includes a noun (itself already something collective, generally speaking) within a class of nouns that share certain properties.[6]

The assignment of gender (S) is an *act of communication* (a message, in fact), which declares that an individual belongs to a particular class of being.

There are thus two reasons not to let oneself be misled by words: gender (S) is not the same as gender (L); assignment (S) is not the same as assignment (L).

---

5 [*Trans.*: see note 3.]
6 It is to be noted that in certain countries the registration of a birth may involve other categories than that of gender (S): racial assignment ("white"), religious assignment (Catholic, Muslim, no religion, etc.), racial-religious assignment, etc.

5. – Having cleared the field, let us try to draw some positive conclusions about the notion of gender (L), taking it, as does La Grasserie, in the enlarged sense of linguistic classes.

THESE CONCLUSIONS ARE PROVISIONAL AND open to further enrichment in the light of more extensive information. In particular we would have to take account of a second article by La Grasserie: "La catégorie psychologique de la classification, révélée par le langage" (1904). What a surprise it is to bring this author back to light and to see how between his two articles he moves from the general problem of classification to a piece specifically on sexuality (Freud's *Three Essays* was published in 1905!).[7]

FOR MY PART, I SHALL use the term "gender (L)" in the general sense of "a category of classification revealed by language," including all the classes of substantives of which La Grasserie speaks, whether or not the language in question requires "agreement."

---

[7]   Raoul de la Grasserie (b. 1839 d. 1914) was a Doctor of Law and a judge at many tribunals in Brittany. He was a member of the Society de linguistique de Paris and of many other learned societies. The author of numerous books and articles (more than 200 titles) on law, sociology, linguistics, psychology and philosophy, he was held in unanimous regard in his own era: "He is to be classed among those who tried to found a new philosophy—not a general philosophy, but a philosophy within each specific science—and to bring out the laws which govern the observation of facts, and create from them a precise synthesis" (Carnoy 1903–1909).

I. La Grasserie and Corbett agree in saying that genders (L):

— are not limited to the sexual domain. The sexed classification may even be absent;

— can be multiple;

— often include a "residual" category: "All the rest."

II. La Grasserie links gender to an "instinct for classification." He analyzes this instinct in terms of a transposition of "kinship in man" into a "kinship among objects" (1898, 596).

Language would then be a revealer of, or a "litmus test" for, this instinct: "Psychic need becomes grammatical need"; "Grammar translates the idea, just as the idea translates the object" (ibid.).

(With this idea of *kinship* between things—of a passage from families of people to families of things—we find a prefiguring of Lévi-Strauss [1968]).

III. La Grasserie tries to bring order to this often dense multiplicity of classifications by distinguishing between

— concrete classifications, and

— abstract classifications.

His definition of *"concrete" classifications*, if taken

literally, could seem absurd. How could certain peoples "limit themselves strictly to what is individual"? How could one have "languages devoid of all classification"? Isn't the substantive itself a classification? If Chinese has no word for "brother" but only "older" and "younger," there are, at least, those two classes! (ibid., 598).

What La Grasserie seems to want to say by means of this distinction is:

a.   that certain languages—those said to be without classification—do not go beyond the substantive, that is to say do not go so far as to have a class of classes;

b.   that at a level which is already superior to the absence of classification, *concrete classification* proceeds, so to speak, little by little, by means of analogy between the members of the class (and perhaps also by contiguity), but without logical opposition, without thinking of the exclusion between classes.

Concrete classification would be "down to earth" (ibid., 610). According to our own terminology, this would be a classification in terms of *diversity* and not a classification by *difference*. In my view, this would be a new reason for a *rapprochement* with Lévi-Strauss, as much with the notion of the "savage mind" as with his revitalised conception of "totemism" (1963).

According to La Grasserie, the concrete classifications

could be:

"objective": aimed at identifying "kinship" among objects or actions (might we say "metaphoric"?);

"subjective": that is, those which "are connected to a part of the human body, either as an object, as an instrument, or as a movement of the body" (ibid., 608) (might we say "metonymic"?)

IV. — Part II (ibid., 610ff) deals with *abstract classification*. The term *"difference"* appears immediately, which is a good confirmation of our hypothesis: *abstract classification* is that which is formulated more or less in terms of differences, or which at least aims towards difference.

La Grasserie proposes a typology of abstract classifications:

1st) The *vitalist classification* into animate and inanimate.

2nd) The *rationalist* one, into beings with and without reason.

3rd) The *hominist* one, between human and non-human beings.

4th) The *virilist* one, between male humans and other beings.

5th) The *intensivist* one, between strong beings and weak beings.

6th) The *gradualist* one, between diminutive and augmentative beings.

7th) The *masculinist* one, between male beings and all the other beings.

8th) The *sexualist* one, between masculine, feminine and asexual

Corbett refers to La Grasserie and raises only relatively minor objections to this classification.

V. — One of the advantages of La Grasserie's work is to show that there is a kind of *evolution* and a trend in the history of classifications. The "*vitalist*" classification (animate—inanimate) would be one of the most primitive.

The "sexualist" classification, on the other hand, would be the one toward which the movement of civilization tends:

This vitalist distinction is the most solidly grounded; we find it, combined with others, in most of the Caucasian languages; indeed, it is founded on movement, one of the most general and most important of the physical factors. Because of its clarity it seems preferable even to the sexualist classification; for the *vitalist* classification encompasses all beings, which it divides up more equally and according to a positive classification, whereas in order to include all beings the *sexualist* classification must institute a negative category, the neuter or asexual. So the vitalist classification could have been adopted by more civilised peoples and to better advantage. However, the opposite occurred, the vitalist classification remained restricted to peoples with an inferior civilization, while those with a superior civilization adopted the sexualist classification (1898, 616).

VI. — The *sexualist* classification often includes three genders: masculine, feminine, neuter. Neuter being the asexual and not the inanimate (ibid., 618).

VII.— So according to La Grasserie again, there would be:

a. A general evolution of "vitalism" toward "sexualism."

b. Some superimpositions of one system over another, and some survivals—in particular, the survival of the inanimate classification within sexualism.

c. "*Some usurpations, or rather, some expansions*" or "*invasions*" (ibid., 614)

In particular: "within the sexualist classification, one endeavours to give a grammatical gender to many objects which do not naturally possess one" (ibid., 618).

This happens according to two mechanisms:
— a "psychological" mechanism: semantic analogies (a certain object resembles the masculine or the feminine)

— a "morphological" mechanism: words ending in *a*, in Latin, are feminine.

VIII. — For my part, I would propose the following idea:

— that because it uses the *difference* of the sexes, the *sexualist system* is the one which lends itself best to a rigorous classification; this is probably by virtue of the binary logic (phallic–castrated) to which this difference lends itself;

— that, paradoxically, it is also the one which lends itself most to *usurpations* of territory between genders: whether it be the usurpation by masculine/ feminine difference, which, in French for example, has almost entirely overrun the territory of the neuter; or whether it be the encroachment of one gender upon another. This latter usurpation is most often, but not always, the usurpation of the feminine gender by the masculine gender, on the grounds that the masculine gender is "unmarked" (*Madame le ministre*, etc.).[8]

On the other hand, in French the word "*personne*," which is feminine, is said to be "unmarked," while in German *Mädchen* is neuter (L) but feminine (S).

---

[8]   [*Trans.*: Laplanche's parenthesis gives an example of standard French linguistic practice whereby a grammatically masculine professional title (*le ministre*) retains its grammatical gender even when collocated with *madame* to indicate that the holder of the post is female.]

To return to assignment (S), the parent at the town hall who is registering the birth of *ein Mädchen*, does not suppose himself to be registering a neuter or asexual being!

So it is only with immense caution that one might suppose the existence of a relationship between this "war of the genders (L)" and a "war of the sexes (S)"! At most one might propose that in the "war of the genders (L)" a certain "masculinism" (whose classification is: the masculine *versus* "the rest") is the "objective ally" of a certain "sexualism" (the only logical difference, since it is clearly symbolizable in terms of the phallus, is sexed difference) and the "objective ally" of the "digital" binarism or system (1 – 0), whose success in the contemporary world is well known.

It is no less remarkable that, just at the point of being "acquired," masculine-feminine difference is immediately doomed to a troubling or contamination. Is this the sign of an instability within binary logic? The victory of a certain "gender trouble" (Judith Butler)?

EPILOGUE

#DOBETTER

#NOTALLPSYCHOANALYSTS

MANY OF OUR PROPOSITIONS IN this volume venture head on into political landmines. We have already addressed why we believe that this is theorizing worth laboring and risking. What we have not yet said explicitly is what inspired it: sitting with real human beings in the consulting room humbles the analyst. One of the reasons we wrote this book is to build the theory we ourselves have also needed in order to work better with patients who are themselves suffering because of the limitations of psychoanalysis and the humans practicing it.

If you are not an analyst it may be hard to appreciate how deeply pleasurable but also how exorbitantly difficult clinical work is. Of the many aspects of this we want to single out, one is especially relevant to this volume. Despite yourself, your best intentions, how earnestly you try to get it right, you will fail. Sometimes, you know why and sometimes not; sometimes you catch it early, sometimes you stay in your mess for a while. If you are going to join the patient rather than stay in the safe domain of your own rendering of what's unfolding in the room, you are taking risks: sometimes they pay off, and in some instances, they don't. This, of course, has considerably different implications for the patient, who is clearly more vulnerable, but it is not at all easy for the analyst either. Sometimes you can work from within this failure, sometimes not.

An example: In the early stages of my work with a trans woman, I (AS) used words for her body that she had never introduced and that did not, in fact, describe how she understood her libidinal embodiment: this was not because I didn't "know" better than to do that, I did. Rather, it was because of how *I* found myself responding to my patient's transfemininity, how *I* was interrupted by what our contact had roused in myself. My patient was sturdy enough to express her upset right then and there; I was grateful, I apologized, and it was, of course, not enough. She also didn't want to talk about it more, as was her right: so I sat back, not forcing that conversation simply because *I* felt awful about my phrasing. It literally took us years before we were *organically* able to talk about the shadow that moment had cast on the treatment, and the distrust in me that it understandably baked into the process. "Why stay?" I asked this patient, when we were finally able to discuss it. "Because this treatment was otherwise helping, and because I could see you were trying," my patient replied. Think about this: staying for years with a therapist who has hurt you, giving them and the treatment a chance.

We mention this example as emblematic of a larger point we want to make to colleagues inexperienced in work with queer and trans patients: *do not for a minute believe that queer and trans patients are categorically impulsive, impatient, and disinterested in long-term treatments, as some of our colleagues pronounce* (Bell, in Blass, Bell, and Saketopoulou, 2021).

Many scholars doing work in queer and trans studies—and gender and sexuality studies more broadly—are, however, not just disinterested in psychoanalysis, but actively antagonistic to its domain. There is no way around the fact that some despise our field, write in an anti-psychoanalytic way, or are otherwise vocal about finding analytic thinking irrelevant to ongoing developments in trans and queer studies. There are several reasons for this: First of all, as we hope we have shown, psychoanalysis has well earned its bad reputation, which does not only refer to sins of the past. As our experience with the *IJP* indicates, psychoanalysis continues to be conservative (seeking to conserve itself rather than be transformed), anxious, and often damning of queerness and gender expansiveness *in the present*. Some of the analysts most publicly vocal in this domain, whose work is visible, public-facing, and materially damaging, were key players in the closing down of the Gender Identity Development Service at the Tavistock clinic in London. This conservativism is not only a European problem either.[1] Our experience speaking

---

[1] This is not to diminish the fact that, as anyone living or working in Europe knows, a trans affirming attitude is so rare and so unlikely in psychoanalysis as to be the rarest of exceptions.

to analysts nationally and AS's extensive background in conducting faculty workshop trainings tell us that this is a problem on this side of the ocean as well.

Secondly, because the majority of analytic writings are transphobic, and uniformly so in the most established, older work, it is also what one is most likely to come up against when first reading, researching, and reviewing the literature. Most of the classics are embarrassing (and we have noted in our preface that even Jean Laplanche, on whom *Gender Without Identity* has relied, would need some revisions in this regard). Once the discipline has been marked as prejudiced, as psychoanalysis has been *and for good reason*, reversing public opinion is not easy. This is another way of saying that we all have considerable work ahead of us to do. And that we should do it.

Third, and we say this as clinicians, some of these authors, many of whom are themselves trans or nonbinary, have been so personally harmed by transphobic attitudes on the couch that this trauma casts all psychoanalytic literature into suspicion, as if there are no analysts writing differently about transness. We don't blame anyone who is so burnt that they need to call out psychoanalysis again and again.

There do now exist bodies of analytic theory, however, many of them cited throughout this volume, that are not steeped in anti-transness. And we are also aware of non-analytic authors who are in fact familiar with more recent, trans-affirming writings, and who systematically do not cite them. We can imagine many reasons for that, but the point we want to make here is that a wholesale disparaging of psychoanalysis is not just problematic from a scholarly standpoint, it also gives up on a resource that can appreciably enhance queer and trans formulations. Psychoanalysis, perhaps more than any other discourse, is capable of navigating nuance and offering depth to think about how gender and sexuality accrue their psychic density, how they come undone and get redone.

That said, in seeking to lift up trans- and queer-affirming resources within psychoanalysis, we are decidedly not advocating for a "both sides" scholarly approach. It is time for analysts and therapists to stop debating trans people's right to exist, which is what we *actually* do when we question whether gender nonconformity is but a manifestation of something else, when all gender, as we have been arguing throughout *Gender Without Identity*, is a manifestation of something else. Such conversations are not only damaging, they also siphen off time and energy from the work we *need* to be doing to think better and to develop an ethos of deep care for queer and trans life. We thus ask our colleagues to resist the siren call of "all opinions matter." Yes, all opinions can be expressed, but we need to become more discerning about whose opinions matter and why, and which can and should be summarily dismissed. A psychoanalysis that becomes hegemonic and legislative is not a psychoanalysis worth saving. Idealization aside (ours included), analysts, like all other humans, are flawed and fearful. Whatever we keep radical we do at a cost, and our hope is that our colleagues dare to pay the price.

More than anything, our hope is that the thinking dared in these pages will have contributed to a psychoanalytic world that openly wants queer and trans people to flourish *in their queerness and transness*. Even, and perhaps especially, those who have been traumatized.

ACKNOWLEDGMENTS

ALL BOOKS ARISE OUT OF the authors' exposure to a variety of discourses, teachings, and influences without which the volume would not have been possible. To try to name all those who should be credited with helping and supporting us in the writing of this volume is a futile endeavor. We would have to recognize those treasured mentors who met our limitations with patience and generosity, and who pushed us, trusting that we would not break, and those who dared break us a little bit; to identify every book that taught us about our subject matters and each volume that educated us in *how* to think; to note individual teachers who broke things down for us and the select clinical supervisors who shaped our sensibilities; to acknowledge all of our activist colleagues whose courage and determination strengthened our resolve to say things that are difficult, to risk upsetting people and institutions; to mention students whose appetite for knowledge held our feet to the fire; to list quotidian encounters that, however small, left an imprint on us that haunted us, galvanizing us to develop or abandon an idea. Even more substantively: confidentiality forbids us from thanking publicly the many patients who, laying on our couches or sitting on our chairs, taught us, sat with our errors, called us out, hung in there while they—and we—figured it out. For those who didn't make it, for whom the process was too difficult, for which our own failures made it too hard, for whom the timing was not right: we are sorry. Please try again; you deserve more, and you deserve better.

That said, there are specific persons we do need to name and personally thank:

First and foremost, Jonathan House stalwartly welcomed our project and gave it a home in our dream press. Jonathan is proof that the usual argument about psychoanalysts' backwardness (and the notion that many analysts trained as part of an older generation just can't keep up) is itself anachronistic: everyone can do better and everyone should. Thank you, Jonathan, for helping steward this work into the world. And if you ever tire of the whole psychoanalyst/psychiatrist/faculty/supervisor/publishing titan thing, there is a mic for you at every comedy club in the country!

Our trusted friends and valued colleagues, Griffin Hansbury and Jack Pula, read earlier versions of this book, taking time they did not have out of their schedules to make helpful suggestions. While the responsibility for our words is ours alone, our book is stronger because of them.

Activist friends both within and outside psychoanalysis helped support us while we were undergoing the bizarre experience the *IJP* put us through. Lara Sheehi and Stephen Sheehi listened carefully and gave steadying advice. Their knowledge, garnered through resistances they have themselves encountered in their fight for the liberation of Palestine, was always thoughtful and caring. In addition to having helped establish the S&GDSC and the first Tiresias

Prize within the auspices of the IPA, Marco Posadas lent us more than an ear and a hand: he tirelessly helped us navigate the disorientation institutional politics often create, reminding us that the feeling of confusion is not a side-effect but part of orthodoxy's method: the wearing down of queer subjects. Thanks also to Leticia Glocer Fiorini and to the IPA's Committee on Sexual and Gender Diversity Studies for their work around the Tiresias prize.

Much appreciation to our copy-editor extraordinaire, Gina Atkinson (few could match our obsessionality, and we are fortunate Gina surpassed it!), our care-full development editor Diana Whitney, and our talented (and *patient*!) cover designer, Vasiliki Kiparissi. Stephan Trano kept all his promises and exceeded our hopes, making the production phase of this project an unusually smooth experience. Giannis Michalopoulos provided all the background logistical and life support that writing a book requires. Γιάννη μας, we appreciate you.

From A.S.: Writing a book we did not intend to write meant that we had to find time we had not budgeted, and that means that it had to be wrested from our personal lives. When the need for this book arose, I had just finished my first book, *Sexuality Beyond Consent: Risk, Race, Traumatophilia*. That process ended with a promise to myself not to write another book, ever. This promise had to be broken (Sam and Chaka, I deserve all the flack!). Having to then delve into another book back-to-back was nothing less than daunting, not to mention depleting. And I would not have embarked on this book with anyone but Ann, whose brilliance and deep knowledge of psychoanalysis are matched only by her fierce political commitments. Lucky me, the height of the *IJP* debacle also found me in the company of the most excellent and fierce dykes Nancy Papanthanasiou and Elena Olga Christidi, who lavished me with equal measures of care and determination. Thank you, Nancy and Elena, for letting me use so much of our vacation time talking and thinking about queerness, politics, and psychoanalysis. Sophia Ploumaki offered solidity and anchoring along several stages of this process. Who would have known, Σοφία μου, when our paths diverged upon leaving Greece, how things would turn out? Thank you, my friend, for your sage advice and for your steady presence. Nikol Delimari, Anna Bondy-Fotiou, and Stella Hatzidelou were my first teachers in gender, and I owe mine to them. Thank you, φιλενάδες μου, for taking me in, thank you for seeing me through.

From AP: Battling the *IJP* is nothing compared to fighting nursing homes. As emails were flying back and forth with the *IJP* and amidst zoom calls across time zones, I was also preoccupied with eldercare. For bolstering and loving counsel during this period, I am grateful to Janet Jakobsen and to Karen Shimakawa. My parents Betty and Ralph have given me many things in life, including generatively mixed messages about gender – what good fortune to be their child. And I wouldn't have wanted, let alone been able, to think or write or dare this accidental book with anyone but Avgi. She is, words fail me, a force.

Finally, we ended up writing this book only because of the *IJP*'s dramatic retraction of its publication commitment to us and to the Sexual and Gender Diversity Studies Committee of the International Psychoanalytical Association. Thanks are thus owed to them as well: both genuine thanks (our essay has greatly benefitted from their editorial feedback) and bittersweet ones (it didn't have to be this way). To the *IJP* editors: we genuinely hope that your journal is able to let itself mutate so that it may survive. It would be a loss for psychoanalysis if it didn't. It is not too late for you to turn this around. But you will not be able to do this alone or without consultation. Remember that the journal is bigger than its masthead, that it has too long a history and too large an influence, that it belongs to all of psychoanalysis, and that you owe it to the field, to analysts, *and to our patients* to stop resisting change and to embrace it. We wish you courage.

REFERENCES

Alpert, Rebecca, ed. 2000. *Voices of the Religious Left: A Contemporary Sourcebook.* Philadelphia: Temple University Press.

Amin, Kadji. 2022. "We Are All Nonbinary: A Brief History of Accidents." *Representations* 158 (1): 106–119.

———— 2023. "Trans Negative Affect." In *The Routledge Companion to Gender and Affect,* edited by T. Reeser, 33–42. New York: Routledge.

Apprey, Maurice. 2014. "A Pluperfect Errand: A Turbulent Return to Beginnings in the Transgenerational Transmission of Destructive Aggression." *Free Associations* 15 (2): 16–29.

Aron, Lewis. 2001. *A Meeting of Minds: Mutuality in Psychoanalysis.* Hillsdale: The Analytic Press.

Aron, Lewis, and Starr, Karen 2013. *A Psychotherapy for the People: Towards a Progressive Psychoanalysis.* New York: Routledge.

Ashley, Florence. (forthcoming). "What Is It Like to Have a Gender Identity?" *MIND.*

———— 2022. "Interrogating Gender-Exploratory Therapy." *Perspectives on Psychological Science* (September 6). https://doi.org/10.1177/17456916221102.

Aulagnier, Piera. 1975. *The Violence of Interpretation: From Pictogram to Statement.* Hove, East Sussex: Brunner-Routledge, 2011.

Baron, Dennis. 2018. "A Brief History of Singular 'They.'" OED.com. https://public.oed.com/blog/a-brief-history-of-singular-they/#.

Barringer, M. N., and Gay, David A. 2017. "Happily Religious: The Surprising Sources of Happiness Among Lesbian, Gay, Bisexual, and Transgender Adults." *Sociological Inquiry* 87 (1): 75–96.

de Beauvoir, Simone. 1949. *The Second Sex,* translated by H. M. Parshley. London: Picador, 1988.

Beckstead, A. Lee. 2012. "Can We Change Sexual Orientation?" *Archives of Sexual Behavior* 41 (1): 121–34.

Bell, David. 2020. "First Do No Harm." *International Journal of Psychoanalysis* 101 (5): 1031–38.

Benjamin, Jessica. 1991. "Father and Daughter: Identification with Difference." *Psychoanalytic Dialogues* 1: 277–99.

Bey, Marquis. 2020a. *Anarcho-Blackness.* Chico: AK Press.

———— 2020b. *The Problem of the Negro as a Problem for Gender.*

Minneapolis: University of Minnesota Press.

——— 2021. "Re: [No Subject]—On Nonbinary Gender." *Qui Parle* 30 (2): 229–47.

——— 2022. *Cistem Failure: Essays on Blackness and Cisgender.* Durham: Duke University Press.

Blass, Rachel B. 2020. Introduction to "Can We Think Psychoanalytically About Transgenderism?" *International Journal of Psychoanalysis* 101 (5): 1014–18.

Blass, Rachel B., Bell, David, and Saketopoulou, Avgi. 2021. "Can We Think Psychoanalytically About Transgenderism?" An expanded live Zoom debate with David Bell and Avgi Saketopoulou, moderated by Rachel Blass. *International Journal of Psychoanalysis* 102 (5): 968–1000.

Bornstein, Kate. 2016. *Gender Outlaws: On Men, Women, and the Rest of Us.* New York: Vintage.

Boyarin, Daniel. 1997. *Unheroic Conduct: The Rise of Heterosexuality and the Invention of the Jewish Man.* Berkeley: University of California Press.

Boyarin, Daniel, Itzkovitz, Daniel, and Pellegrini, Ann, eds. 2003. *Queer Theory and the Jewish Question.* New York: Columbia University Press.

Brisson, Luc. 2002. *Sexual Ambivalence: Androgyny and Hermaphroditism in Graeco-Roman Antiquity,* translated by Janet Lloyd. Berkeley: University of California Press.

Browning, Deborah L. 2016. "Laplanche: From the Enigmatic Message of the Other to the Unconscious Alterity Within." *Journal of the American Psychoanalytic Association* 64 (5): 1037–49.

Butler, Judith. 1990. *Gender Trouble: Feminism and the Subversion of Identity.* London/New York: Routledge.

——— 1993. *Bodies That Matter: On the Discursive Limits of Sex.* London/New York: Routledge.

Capell, Ezra, and Lang, Jessica, eds. 2020. *Off the Derech: Leaving Orthodox Judaism.* New York: SUNY Press.

Carnoy, Henry. 1903–1909. *Dictionnaire biographique international des écrivains, vols. 1–4.* Paris: G. Olms, 1987.

Cavanagh, Sheila L. 2016. "Transsexuality as a Sinthome: Bracha L. Ettinger and the Other (Feminine) Sexual Difference." *Studies in Gender and Sexuality* 17 (1): 27–44.

——— 2018. "Transgender Embodiment: A Lacanian Approach."

Psychoanalytic Review 105 (3): 303–27.

Chiland, Colette. 2000. "The Psychoanalyst and the Transsexual Patient." *International Journal of Psychoanalysis* 81 (1): 21–35.

Chu, Andrea Long. 2018. "Opinion: My New Vagina Won't Make Me Happy." *The New York Times* (November 24). https://www.nytimes.com/2018/11/24/opinion/sunday/vaginoplasty-transgender-medicine.html.

Clarke, Jessica A. 2015. "Against Immutability." *Yale Law Journal* 125 (2): 2–102.

Coates, Susan. 1990. "Ontogenesis of Boyhood Gender Identity Disorder." *Journal of the American Academy of Psychoanalysis and Dynamic Psychiatry* 18: 414–38.

Coates, Susan, and Moore, Mary Sue. 1998. "The Complexity of Early Trauma: Representation and Transformation." In *A Stranger in My Own Body: Atypical Gender Identity Development and Mental Health,* edited by D. DiCeglie, 39–62. London: Karnac.

Corbett, Greville. 1991. *Gender.* Cambridge: Cambridge University Press.

Corbett, Ken. 2001. "More Life." *Psychoanalytic Dialogues* 11: 313–35.

———. 2009. *Boyhoods: Rethinking Masculinities.* New Haven: Yale University Press.

———. 2011. "Gender Regulation." *Psychoanalytic Quarterly* 80 (2): 441–59.

Crenshaw, Kimberlé. 1989. "Demarginalizing the Intersection of Race and Sex: A Black Feminist Critique of Antidiscrimination Doctrine, Feminist Theory and Antiracist Politics." *University of Chicago Legal Forum 1,* Article 8, 139–67. http://chicagounbound.uchicago.edu/uclf/vol1989/iss1/8.

Crosby, Christina. 2016. *A Body Undone: Living on After Great Pain.* New York: New York University Press.

D'Angelo, Roberto. 2020. "The Man I Am Trying to Be Is Not Me." *International Journal of Psychoanalysis* 101 (5): 951–70.

D'Angelo, Roberto, Marchiano, Lisa, and Gorin, Shlomit. 2022. "Response to Book Review Essay, 'On Trying to Pass Off Transphobia as Psychoanalysis and Cruelty as "Clinical Logic,"' by Avgi Saketopoulou." *Psychoanalytic Quarterly* 91 (3): 591–94.

Dejours, Christophe. 1986. *Le Corps d'Abord.* Paris: Payot, 2001.

Dimen, Muriel. 1991. "Deconstructing Difference: Gender, Splitting, and Transitional Space." *Psychoanalytic Dialogues* 1: 335–52.

————, ed. 2011. *With Culture in Mind: Psychoanalytic Stories.* New York: Routledge.

Dimen, Muriel, and Goldner, Virginia. 2006. "Gender and Sexuality." In *Textbook of Psychoanalysis,* edited by E. S. Person, A. M. Cooper, and G. O. Gabbard, 93–114. Washington, DC: American Psychiatric Publishing.

Dornes, Martin. 1996. "La théorie de Margaret Mahler reconsidérée." *Psyche* 50 (11). Reprinted in *Psychanalyse et Psychologie du Première âge.* Paris: Presses Universitaires de France, 2002.

Dutta, Aniruddha. 2018. "Allegories of Gender: Transgender Autology Versus Transracialism." *Atlantis: Critical Studies in Gender Culture and Social Justice* 39 (2): 86–98.

Elise, Dianne. 2001. "Unlawful Entry: Male Fears of Psychic Penetration." *Psychoanalytic Dialogues* 11 (4): 499–531.

Enke, Finn. 2012. "The Education of Little Cis: Cisgender and the Discipline of Opposing Bodies." In *Transfeminist Perspectives in and beyond Transgender and Gender Studies,* edited by Finn Enke, 60–77. Philadelphia: Temple University Press.

Evans, Susan, and Evans, Marcus. 2021. *A Therapeutic Model for Working with Children, Adolescents and Young Adults.* Oxfordshire: Phoenix Publishing House.

Evzonas, Nicolas. 2020. "Gender and 'Race' Enigmatic Signifiers: How the Social Colonizes the Unconscious." *Psychoanalytic Inquiry* 40 (8): 636–56.

Fader, Ayala. 2020. *Hidden Heretics: Jewish Doubt in the Digital Age.* Princeton: Princeton University Press.

Farley, Lisa, and Kennedy, R. M. 2020. "Transgender Embodiment as an Appeal to Thought: A Psychoanalytic Critique of 'Rapid Onset Gender Dysphoria.'" *Studies in Gender and Sexuality* 21 (3): 155–72.

Florence, Jean. 1978. *L'Identification Dans la Théorie Freudienne.* Brussels: Universités Saint-Louis.

Foucault, Michel. 1970. *The Order of Things.* New York: Pantheon.

———— 1978. *The History of Sexuality, Vol. I: An Introduction.* New York: Vintage Books.

———— 1981. "Practicing Criticism." In *Politics, Philosophy, Culture: Interviews and Other Writings, 1977–1984,* edited by Lawrence Kritzman, 152–56. New York: Routledge, 1988.

Frank, Gillian A., Moreton, Bethany, and White, Heather R., eds. 2018. *Devotions and Desires: Histories of Sexuality and Religion in the Twentieth-Century United States*. Chapel Hill: University of North Carolina Press.

Freud, Sigmund. 1900. *The Interpretation of Dreams. Standard Edition,* 4 and 5.

———— 1905. "Three Essays on the Theory of Sexuality." *Standard Edition,* 7.

———— 1908. "On the Sexual Theories of Children." *Standard Edition,* 9.

———— 1909. "Analysis of a Phobia in a Five-Year-Old Boy." *Standard Edition,* 10.

———— 1911. "Psycho-Analytic Notes on an Autobiographical Account of a Case of Paranoia (Dementia Paranoides)." *Standard Edition,* 12.

———— 1912. "On the Universal Tendency to Debasement in the Sphere of Love." *Standard Edition,* 11.

———— 1921. *Group Psychology and the Analysis of the Ego. Standard Edition,* 18.

———— 1923. *The Ego and the Id. Standard Edition,* 19.

———— 1925. "Some Psychical Consequences of the Anatomical Distinction Between the Sexes." *Standard Edition,* 19.

———— 1933. "Lecture 33: Femininity." *New Introductory Lectures on Psycho-Analysis. Standard Edition,* 22.

———— 1937. "Analysis Terminable and Interminable." *Standard Edition,* 23.

Garfinkle, Michael, Gentile, Jill, Litowitz, Bonnie E., Pellegrini, Ann, Sheehi, Lara, Wilson, Mitchell, and Zeavin, Lynne. 2019. "What Can I Say? Contested Words and Contested Thoughts in the Contemporary Moment." *Journal of the American Psychoanalytic Association* 67 (4): 655–97.

Geller, Jay. 2007. *On Freud's Jewish Body: Mitigating Circumcisions*. New York: Fordham University Press.

Gherovici, Patricia. 2010. *Please Select Your Gender: From the Invention of Hysteria to the Democratizing of Transgenderism*. New York: Routledge.

———— 2017. *Transgender Psychoanalysis: A Lacanian Perspective on Sexual Difference*. New York/London: Routledge.

———— 2019. "Transgender Expressions and Psychosis: Towards an Ethics of Sexual Difference." *British Journal of Psychotherapy* 35 (3): 417–30.

Gill-Peterson, Jules. 2018. *Histories of the Transgender Child*. Minneapolis: University of Minnesota Press.

———— 2021. "When Did We Become Cis?" https://sadbrowngirl. substack.com/p/when-did-we-become-cis.

———— 2022. *Gender Reveal* Podcast. Episode 126 (July 4), https:// www.genderpodcast.com, 62 mins.

Gill-Peterson, Jules, and Saketopoulou, Avgi. 2022. "Exposing Transphobic Legacies, Embracing Trans Life: A Conversation Between Jules Gill-Peterson and Avgi Saketopoulou." *Couched* Podcast (June 6), https://couchedpodcast.org, 55 mins.

Gilman, Sander. 1991. *The Jew's Body*. New York: Routledge.

———— 1993. *Freud, Race, and Gender*. Princeton: Princeton University Press.

Glocer Fiorini, Leticia. 2015. *La diferencia sexual en debate: Cuerpos, deseos y ficciones*. Buenos Aires: Lugar Editorial.

Goldner, Virginia (2011). Trans: Gender in Free Fall. *Psychoanalytic Dialogues* 21: 159-171.

González, Francisco. 2019. "Writing Gender with Sexuality: Reflections on the Diaries of Lou Sullivan." *Journal of the American Psychoanalytic Association* 67 (1): 59–82.

Gortais, Jean. 1987. "Le concept de symbiose en psychanalyse." *Psychanalyse à l'Université* 12 (6): 201–58.

Gozlan, Oren. 2008. "The Accident of Gender." *Psychoanalytic Review* 95 (4): 541–70.

———— 2014. *Transexuality and the Art of Transitioning: A Lacanian Approach*. London: Routledge.

———— 2018. "From Continuity to Contiguity: A Response to the Fraught Temporality of Gender." *Psychoanalytic Review* 105 (1): 1–29.

———— 2019. "Transsexuality as an Emotional Situation: Aesthetics and a State of Mind: A Question of Difference." http://www. publicseminar.org/2019/06/transsexuality-as-an-emotional-situation-aesthetics-and-a-state-of-mind.

———— 2022. "Gender as Lint Collector." *Psychoanalytic Study of the Child* 75 (1): 173–8.

Gozlan, Oren, Osserman, Jordan, Silber, Laurel, Wallerstein, Hannah, Watson, Eve, and Wiggins, Tobias 2022. "Transgender Children: From Controversy to Dialogue." *Psychoanalytic Study of the Child*, 75 (1): 198–214.

de la Grasserie, Raoul. 1898. "La catégorie psychologique de la classification, révélée par le langage." *Revue philosophique* 45: 594–624.

Grossmark, Robert (2018). *The Unobtrusive Relational Analyst: Explorations in Psychoanalytic Companioning*. New York: Routledge.

Halley, Janet E. 1994. "Sexual Orientation and the Politics of Biology: A Critique of the Argument from Immutability." *Stanford Law Review* 46 (3): 503–68.

Hansbury, Griffin. 2011. "King-Kong and Goldilocks: Imagining Trans Masculinities Through the Trans-Trans Dyad." *Psychoanalytic Dialogues* 21 (2): 210–20.

———— 2017a. "The Masculine Vaginal: Working with Queer Men's Embodiment at the Transgender Edge." *Journal of the American Psychoanalytic Association* 65 (6): 1009–31.

———— 2017b. "Unthinkable Anxieties: Reading Transphobic Countertransferences in a Century of Psychoanalytic Writing. *Transgender Studies Quarterly* 4 (3-4): 384–404.

Hansbury, Griffin, and Saketopoulou, Avgi. 2022. "Sissy Dance $1: The More and More of Gender." *Psychoanalytic Review* 109 (3): 227–56.

Harris, Adrienne. 2009. *Gender as Soft Assembly*. New York: Routledge.

Hirata, Helena, Laborie, Françoise, Ledoaré, Hélène, and Senotier, Danièle. 2000. *Dictionnaire critique du féminisme*. Paris: Presses Universitaires de France.

Jakobsen, Janet R., and Pellegrini, Ann. 2004. *Love the Sin: Sexual Regulation and the Limits of Religious Tolerance*. Boston: Beacon Press.

Joynt, Chase, director. 2022. *Framing Agnes*. New York: Kino Lorber (December 2).

Kernberg, Otto. 1995. *Love Relations*. New Haven: Yale University Press.

Kubie, Lawrence. 1974. "The Drive to Become Both Sexes." *Psychoanalytic Quarterly* 43 (3): 349–426.

Lacan, Jacques. 1959. "On a Question Prior to any Possible Treatment of Psychosis." In *Écrits*, translated by Bruce Fink. New York: W. W. Norton.

Ladin, Joy. 2018. *The Soul of the Stranger: Reading God and Torah from a*

Transgender Perspective. Waltham: Brandeis University Press.

Langer, S. J. 2016. "Trans Bodies and the Failure of Mirrors." *Studies in Gender and Sexuality* 17 (4): 306–16.

Laplanche, Jean. 1970. *Life and Death in Psychoanalysis*, edited by John Fletcher. Baltimore: Johns Hopkins Press.

———— 1980. *Problématiques I: L'Angoisse*. Paris: Presses Universitaires de France.

———— 1980. *Problématiques II: Castrations-Symbolisations*. Paris: Presses Universitaires de France.

———— 1980. *Problématiques III: La Sublimation*. Paris: Presses Universitaires de France.

———— 1981. *Problématiques IV: L'Inconscient et le ça*. Paris: Presses Universitaires de France.

———— 1987. *New Foundations for Psychoanalysis*, translated by Jonathan House. New York: The Unconscious in Translation, 2016.

———— 1987. *Problématiques V: Le baquet: Transcendance du Transfert*. Paris: Presses Universitaires de France.

———— 1998/2017. "Time and the Other." In *Après-Coup,* translated by Jonathan House. New York: The Unconscious in Translation.

———— 1999. "Notes on Afterwardsness." In *Essays on Otherness*, edited by John Fletcher. London/New York: Routledge.

———— 2008. *Nouveaux Fondements Pour La Psychoanalyse*. Paris: Presses Universitaires de France.

———— 2011. *Freud and the Sexual: Essays 2000–2006, edited by John Fletcher*. New York: Unconscious in Translation Press.

———— 1992/2020. "Masochism and the General Theory of Seduction." In *The Unfinished Copernican Revolution: Selected Works, 1967-1992*, translated by Luke Thurston. New York: The Unconscious in Translation.

Laplanche, Jean, Fletcher, John, and Osborne, Peter 2000. "Interview with Jean Laplanche: The Other Within." *Radical Philosophy* 102 (July/August): 31–41.

Laplanche, Jean, and Pontalis, Jean-Bertrand. 1973. *The Language of Psychoanalysis*, translated by Donald Nicholson-Smith. London: Hogarth Press.

Lemma, Alessandra. 2018. "Trans-Itory Identities: Some Psychoanalytic Reflections on Transgender Identities." *International Journal of*

Psychoanalysis 99 (5): 1089–1106.

Lévi-Strauss, Claude. 1962. *The Savage Mind*, translated by John Weightman and Doreen Weightman. Chicago: Chicago University Press, 1968.

———— 1962. *Totemism,* translated by Rodney Needham. Boston: Beacon Press, 1963.

Malatino, Hil. 2020. *Trans Care*. Minneapolis, MN: University of Minnesota Press.

———— 2022. *Side Affects: On Being Trans and Feeling Bad*. Minneapolis: University of Minnesota Press.

Matthieu, Nicole-Claude. 1991. "Trois modes de conceptualisation du rapport entre sexe et genre." In *L'Anatomie Politique*. Paris: Côté femmes.

Meanley, Steven, Haberlen, Sabina A., Okafor, Chukwuemeka. N., Brown, Andre, Brennan-Ing, Mark, Ware, Deanna, Egan, James E., Teplin, Linda A., Bolan, Robert K., Friedman, Mackey. R., and Plankey, Michael. W. 2020. "Lifetime Exposure to Conversion Therapy and Psychosocial Health Among Midlife and Older Adult Men Who Have Sex With Men." *Gerontologist* 60 (7): 1291–1302.

Muñoz, Josè Esteban. 2009. *Cruising Utopia: The Then and There of Queer Futurity*. New York: NYU Press.

Oppenheimer, Agnès. 1984. "Le meilleur des mondes possible: à propos du projet de R. Schafer." *Psychanalyse à l'Université* 9 (35): 467–82.

Osborne, Peter. 1996. *A Critical Sense*. London: Routledge.

Osserman, Jordan, and Wallerstein, Hannah. 2022. "Transgender Children: From Controversy to Dialogue." *Psychoanalytic Study of the Child* 75: 159–72.

Pellegrini, Ann. 1997. *Performance Anxieties: Staging Psychoanalysis, Staging Race*. New York: Routledge.

Pellegrini, Ann, and Saketopoulou, Avgi. 2019. "On Taking Sides: They/Them Pronouns, Gender and the Psychoanalyst." http://www.psychoanalysis.today/en-GB/PT-Articles/Pellegrini167541/On-taking-sides-they-them-pronouns,-gender-and-the.aspx.

Perelberg, Rosine J. 2018. "The Riddle of Anxiety: Between the Familiar and the Unfamiliar." *International Journal of Psychoanalysis* 99 (4): 810–27.

Person, Ethel Spector. 1999. *The Sexual Century*. New Haven: Yale

University Press.

Person, Ethel Spector, and Ovesey, Lionel. 1983. "Psychoanalytic Theories of Gender Identity." *Journal of the American Academy of Psychoanalysis* 11 (2): 203–26.

Povinelli, Elizabeth A. 2006. *The Empire of Love: Toward a Theory of Intimacy, Genealogy, and Carnality*. Durham: Duke University Press.

Preciado, Paul. 2019. "Intervention, Femmes en Psychanalyse." *Journées 49 de l'ECF (Ecole de la Cause Freudienne)*. https://www.youtube.com/watch?v=vqNJbZR_QZ4.

Pula, Jack. 2015. "Understanding Gender Through the Lens of Transgender Experience." *Psychoanalytic Inquiry* 35 (8): 809–22.

Reiche, Reimut. 1997. "Gender ohne Sex: Geschichte, Funktion und Funktionswandel des begriffs." *Psyche* 51 (9/10): 926–57.

Riviere, Joan. 1929. "Womanliness as Masquerade." *International Journal of Psychoanalysis* 10: 303–13.

Roiphe, Herman, and Galenson, Eleanor. 1981. *Infantile Origins of Sexual Identity*. Madison: International Universities Press.

Rosik, Christopher H., Lefevor, G. Tyler, McGraw, James S., and Beckstead, A. Lee. 2021. "Is Conservative Religiousness Inherently Associated with Poorer Health for Sexual Minorities?" *Journal of Religion and Health* 61 (4): 1–21.

Rubin, Gayle. 1992. "Of Catamites and Kings: Reflections on Butch, Gender, and Boundaries." In *The Persistent Desire: A Femme-Butch Reader*, edited by J. Nestle, 466–82. Boston: Alyson Publications.

Saketopoulou, Avgi. 2011. "Minding the Gap: Race and Class in Clinical Work with Gender Variant Children." *Psychoanalytic Dialogues* 21 (2): 192–209.

——— 2014. "Mourning the Body as Bedrock: Developmental Considerations in Treating Transsexual Patients Analytically." *Journal of the American Psychoanalytic Association* 62 (5): 773–805.

——— 2017a. "Between Freud's Second and Third Essays on Sexuality: Commentary on Hansbury." *Journal of the American Psychoanalytic Association* 65 (6): 1033–48.

——— 2017b. "Structured Like Culture: Laplanche and the Translation of Enigma." *DIVISION/Review* 17: 51–52.

——— 2020a. "How the World Becomes Bigger; Implantation, Intromission and the Après-Coup: Discussion of Jonathan House's Paper 'Après-Coup.'" In *The Unconscious: Contemporary*

Refractions in Psychoanalysis, edited by P. Sauvayre and D. Braucher, 174–84. New York: Routledge.

———— 2020b. "Thinking Psychoanalytically, Thinking Better; Reflections on Transgender." *International Journal of Psychoanalysis* 101 (5): 1019–30.

———— 2022. "On Trying to Pass Off Transphobia as Psychoanalysis and Cruelty as 'Clinical Logic.'" Psychoanalytic Quarterly 91 (1): 177–90.

————2023a. "Anti-Racist Racism: Trauma, Traumatism, Traumatophilia." *Journal of the American Psychoanalytic Association.*

———— 2023b. *Sexuality Beyond Consent: Risk, Race, Traumatophilia.* New York: NYU Press.

Salamon, Gayle. 2010. *Assuming a Body: Transgender and Rhetorics of Materiality.* New York: Columbia University Press.

———— 2014. "The Dignity of Belief." *Undecidable Unconscious: A Journal of Deconstruction and Psychoanalysis* 1: 113–18.

———— 2018. *The Life and Death of Latisha King: A Critical Phenomenology of Transphobia.* New York: New York University Press.

Scarfone, Dominique. 2010. "In the Hollow of Transference: The Analyst's Position Between Activity and Passivity." *Sitegeist: A Journal of Psychoanalysis and Philosophy* 4 (10): 7–20.

———— 2013. "The Disappearance of the Shadows." *Contre-jour, cahiers littéraires* 30: 143–7.

———— 2014. "The *Three Essays* and the Meaning of the Infantile Sexual in Psychoanalysis." *Psychoanalytic Quarterly* 83: 327–44.

———— 2015. *Laplanche, an Introduction.* New York: The Unconscious in Translation.

———— 2016. "Fantasme et processus de fantasmatisation." *Revue Française de Psychosomatique* 50 (2): 47–68.

———— 2019. "The *Sexual* and Psychical Reality." *International Journal of Psychoanalysis* 100 (6): 1248–55.

———— 2021. "Speech and the Drives: Psychoanalysis and Living Systems." Sandor Radò Lecture, Association for Psychoanalytic Medicine, Columbia University, New York, May 3.

———— (forthcoming). *The Reality of the Message: A Translational Model of the Psyche.* New York: Unconscious in Translation Press.

Schevers, Ky. 2020. "Detransition as Conversion Therapy: A Survivor

Speaks Out," *Medium*. https://medium.com/an-injustice/detransition-as-conversion-therapy-a-survivor-speaks-out-7abd4a9782fa.

——— . 2022. "Ky Schever's [sic] experience with ideologically driven detransition." https://transsafety.network/posts/ky-schevers-life-in-detransition/.

Sedgwick, Eve Kosofsky. 1990. *The Epistemology of the Closet*. Berkeley: University of California Press.

——— 1991. "How to Bring Your Kids Up Gay." *Social Text* 29: 18–27.

Seidman, Naomi. 2021. "Leaving Orthodoxy, Again." https://www.publicbooks.org/leaving-orthodoxy-again.

——— 2022. "Heretic in the House." Podcast. Shalom Hartman Institute of North America. Written by Naomi Seidman, produced by M. Louis Gordon.

Serano, Julia. 2022. "It's Time to Rethink 'Born This Way,' a Phrase That's Been Key to LGBTQ Acceptance." https://www.salon.com/2022/06/17/its-time-to-rethink-born-this-way-a-phrase-thats-been-key-to-lgbtq-acceptance.

Silverman, Sandra. 2023. "Who's Transitioning? A cisgender analyst working with gender expansive patients," *Psychoanalytic Perspectives* 20 (1): 31-48.

Slomowitz, Alan, and Feit, Alison, eds. 2019. *Homosexuality, Transsexuality, Psychoanalysis and Traditional Judaism*. New York: Routledge.

Snorton, C. Riley. 2017. *Black on Both Sides: A Racial History of Trans Identity*. Minneapolis: University of Minnesota Press

Socarides, Charles. W. 1984. "Infantile Origins of Sexual Identity." *Psychoanalytic Quarterly* 53: 454–59.

Sontag, Susan. 1964. "Notes on 'Camp.'" Reprinted in *Against Interpretation and Other Essays,* 275–92. New York: Anchor Books, 1990.

Spack, Norman. P., Edwards-Leeper, Laura, Feldman, Henry A., Leibowitz, Scott, Mandel, Francie, Diamond, David A., and Vance, Stanley. R. 2012. "Children and Adolescents with Gender Identity Disorder Referred to a Pediatric Medical Center." *Pediatrics* 129: 418–25.

Spillers, Hortense. 1987. "Mama's Baby, Papa's Maybe: An American Grammar Book." *Diacritics* 17 (2): 64–81.

de Spinoza, Benedict. 1677. "Ethics: Demonstrated in Geometrical

Order." In *The Essential Spinoza: Ethics and Related Writings*, translated by Samuel Shirley, edited by Michael L. Morgan. Indianapolis: Hackett Publishing Company, 2006.

Stoller, Robert J. 1964. "A Contribution to the Study of Gender Identity." *International Journal of Psychoanalysis* 45: 220–26.

——— 1966. "The Mother's Contribution to Infantile Transvestic Behavior." *International Journal of Psychoanalysis* 47: 384–95.

——— 1968. *Sex and Gender*. London: Hogarth Press.

——— 1975. *Perversion: The Erotic Form of Hatred*. London: Karnac.

——— 1985. *Presentations of Gender*. New Haven: Yale University Press.

Suchet, Melanie. 2011. "Crossing Over." *Psychoanalytic Dialogues* 21 (2): 172–91.

Turban, Jack. L, Carswell, Jeremi., and Keuroglian, Alex S. 2018. "Understanding Pediatric Patients Who Discontinue Gender-Affirming Hormonal Interventions." *Journal of the American Society for Pediatrics* 172 (10): 963–64.

Turban, Jack L., and Ehrensaft, Diane 2018. "Research Review: Gender Identity in Youth: Treatment Paradigms and Controversies." *Journal of Child Psychology and Psychiatry* 59 (12): 1228–43.

Urquhart, Evan 2021. "An 'Ex-Detransitioner' Disavows the Anti-Trans Movement She Helped Spark." https://slate.com/human-interest/2021/02/detransition-movement-star-ex-gay-explained.html.

Van Haute, Philippe., and Westerink, Herman. 2016. "Sexuality and Its Object in Freud's 1905 Edition of *Three Essays on the Theory of Sexuality*." *International Journal of Psychoanalysis* 97: 563–89.

Versaldi, Guiseppe, and Zani, Angelo Vinconzo 2019. "'Male and Female He Created Them': Towards a Path of Dialogue on the Question of Gender in Education." Vatican City, Congregation for Catholic Education. http://www.educatio.va/content/dam/cec/Documenti/19_0997_INGLESE.pdf.

White, Heather. R. 2015. *Reforming Sodom: Protestants and the Rise of Gay Rights*. Chapel Hill: University of North Carolina Press.

Wiggins, Tobias. 2020. "A Perverse Solution to Misplaced Distress: Trans Subjects and Clinical Disavowal." *Transgender Studies Quarterly* 7 (1): 56–76.

——— 2022. "Listening for Trans Childism in Discursive Concern." *Psychoanalytic Study of the Child* 75 (1): 191–97.